KALEVALA
T A R O T

KALEVALA
T A R O T

Kalervo Aaltonen

Paintings by Taina Pailos

First Edition

Library of Congress Cataloging-in-Publication Data

Aaltonen, Kai Kalervo
  Kalevala Tarot
Paintings by Taina Pailos
English translation Gian Svennevig
Edited in Finnish by Saana Saarinen

ISBN 0-88079-186-1

Library of Congress Catalog Card Number: 95-81656

99 10 9 8 7 6 5 4 3 2 1

Printed in Canada

U.S. GAMES SYSTEMS, INC.
179 Ludlow Street
Stamford, CT 06902 USA

for my sons

JANI and HANS

LIST OF CONTENTS

INTRODUCTION

WHILE LIVING IN YORK, a city in northern England that used to be the site of the Viking settlement Eboracum, Kai Kalervo Aaltonen wrote his first book, on numerology. In York he also became familiar with Viking mythology and with the mysterious and fascinating world of the tarot. He became convinced that all of us should find a means of connecting with the collective consciousness of Humanity—and that we all, each and every one of us, have a different way open to us, the way that will come most naturally to us, that will seem familiar. This realization led to a chain of events, the fruit of which is the Kalevala Tarot.

The tarot has been used as an instrument for therapy and introspection in many different cultures. The Kalevala, in turn, is the Finnish national epic. It, too, has found its way to other cultures—it has been translated into 41 languages. The Kalevala poems speak of the creation of the world and of agriculture, they speak of the forces that form our lives, and of human development.

Having completed his book on runes, Kai Kalervo Aaltonen spoke with the artist Taina Pailos about his idea of creating a tarot deck based on the Kalevala epic. She expressed great interest in the idea and together, one card at a time, they created the Kalevala Tarot—a deck where ancient Finnish mythology comes alive through the powerful symbolism of the tarot.

The mythological world of the Kalevala enhances the tarot deck's qualities—the Kalevala brings a freshness to the tarot symbolism with its primeval cosmology and shamanistic view of humanity.

The Kalevala poems, as did the tarot cards, came into being a very long time ago. Then, knowledge was spread in quite a different way from now—through pictures, songs and religious ceremonies. The Kalevala Tarot is one way of trying to bring that ancient wisdom into the lives of modern man and woman. This wisdom can change and give new meaning to the tasks before us. We need it now, as much as it was needed then—if not more than ever.

The people of the Kalevala are easy for modern men and women to identify with—this is one of the epic's strengths. The characters, their failings and weaknesses, as well as their good points, their victories, their hopes and joys all seem very familiar. There is something universal about them.

On an individual level we often have similar experiences to the different Kaleva Heroes, even in this day and age. Kalevala tells us of the fight for survival, but in a mythological way.

Finland is famous for its sportsmen and women, its composers—and for the Kalevala. The Kalevala has influenced the birth of the Estonian Kalevipoeg, as well as Longfellow's Hiawatha. Indeed, many artists, Finns and non-Finns alike, have used the Kalevala imagery in their art, films, music and plays. Countless Finnish artists have been inspired by the Kalevala; the composer Jean Sibelius and the painter Akseli Gallen-Kallela are two of the most famous ones. In 1993 the opera *Kullervo*, by Aulis Sallinen, had its premier in Los Angeles—it, too, is Kalevala-inspired. In Finland, Kalevala Day is celebrated annually on February 28.

Elias Lönnrot compiled the Kalevala from over 85,000 poems. He was both a doctor, practicing in Kajaani, and a professor of the Finnish language at Helsinki University. He made eleven journeys on foot, and walked about 20,000 kilometers, in order to collect poems for the Kalevala. He also collected a lot of other folklore—the *Kanteletar* and *Suomen*

Kansan Loitsurunoja contain some of this. Lönnrot compiled a Finnish-Swedish Dictionary, as well.

In the years 1822-1831, Elias Lönnrot and the writer Sakari Topelius the older, published ten booklets of folk poetry. This was when the idea began take root in Lönnrot for a Finnish epic on the scale of Homer's *Odyssey*. In the final epic there are 50 poems altogether.

The Kalevala Tarot joins two old mythological worlds together for the first time, the archetypes of which can still be found all around us in the world today. By using the Kalevala Tarot, you will gain entrance into your intuitive world and then perhaps unlock the creative processes of your imagination. The insight these processes will bring to your particular situation will come forth from a fusing of the inner and outer, from you meeting circumstance, from the individual standing alone and in a community. You could call this process Sampo's magic; it is shown in the tarot card of the three stakes.

This book approaches the human situation by using the Kalevala mythology, the tarot symbolism, and the experience of a single individual who uses the cards. The Kalevala expresses the teachings of the community; the tarot symbolizes outside knowledge and the individual herself, inside knowledge.

There are several words in the Finnish language that can be connected, one way or another, to the word *tarot*. Firstly, there is the word *taro,* meaning something like *village* or *neighborhood*. In the tarot cards an imaginary village or community is built where everything that we might meet in reality can be examined. They contain the experiences and the knowledge accumulated in thousands of years and through countless human lives.

In Finland there are also some places with the word *taro* in their names, such as Ylistaro, Alastaro, Haikastaro, Tarola, Tarovaara, Taromäki and Taroniemi.

There is the adjective *tarossa*, which means that something is open, visible, within reach. Using the tarot will, hopefully, bring new things forth, out into the open and within reach—it will make the workings of the unconscious more accessible and throw light on them.

The tarot shows some events and states of mind that most of us will experience at one time or another, that fate will throw our way.

We read about different stages of life and different crises in magazines and novels. We watch movies where people have great adventures, and we gossip incessantly about the people around us. In the tarot cards we can see and read about our very own adventures—we can be the Heroes and Heroines of our own lives.

The Kalevala Tarot shows just how modern and how practical the Kalevala mythology is. It is perfectly suited to the tarot symbolism—so much so that it is almost as if Elias Lönnrot was acquainted with the tarot when he compiled the Kalevala.

The Kalevala Tarot can also be transposed on to the Kabbalah's Tree of Life. The symbol of the Enneagram, George Gurdjieff's and John Godolph Bennet's diagram of the cosmic forces, has much influenced the author of this book.

Scholars of the esoteric, those committed to the spiritual side of life, studying the mystery of Mankind and its place in the Universe, may find new insight and strengthen former insights by using the Kalevala Tarot. The cards can also be used in therapy—those practicing Jungian therapy will find the Kalevala Tarot especially useful.

Last but not least, you "ordinary person," you man or woman on the street—you Tom, Dick or Harry, or Mary, Jane or Susan, as the case may be!—no you aren't, you are not "ordinary." Look into the Kalevala tarot cards and see just how extraordinary your life is.

THE TAROT

THE TAROT, OR TAROC, is a pack of 78 cards. Some of the cards can be divided into suits, just as in a conventional deck of cards. These suits also contain court cards, as in a conventional deck. A conventional deck of cards has 12 of these, whereas a tarot card deck has 16—the additional four are either pages or princesses. The suits with the court cards all belong to the Minor Arcana. You could say that a tarot deck has 22 jokers. These "jokers" all portray different spiritual aspects that are part of being a human being, and are called the Major Arcana.

The origins and history of the tarot are much debated. One school of thought claims the tarot originated in China, India or Persia. It was then introduced to the West through the crusades, or by gypsies. Others believe the tarot originated in Europe—the first mention of the cards in Europe is in 1332 when their usage was forbidden.

When the Major Arcana became part of the tarot deck is also a riddle. However, for at least 500 years the illustrations for the Major Arcana have remained relatively unchanged—it is only recently that many different interpretations of them have been made. It has been said that the tarot cards contain secret knowledge about Ancient Egypt. Some of the symbolism found in them is much the same as in the ancient Persian Mithraic religion, some is the same as was used in Celtic Paganism—indeed, it seems that tarot symbolism has been drawn from many sources.

The tarot deck has symbols for the different aspects and the various stages of a person's life—for all the great moments, from birth to death, the struggles, the joys, the tragedies and the changes we all will have our share of. By using the tarot, a person can lay their life out before them and endeavor to look at it as if from the outside.

Anyone's life holds secrets, both big and little ones. The little secrets of life are hidden in the everyday: work, money, home and relationships. These little secrets are symbolized in the Lesser Mysteries, or Minor Arcana of the tarot deck—"lesser" because the reality we perceive in the material, and in the practicalities of daily life, is only a part and a reflection of a much Greater Mystery. The Minor Arcana is divided into four suits. These symbolize the four elements: fire, water, air and earth. These elements point us to the boundaries of human existence, much in the same way as the weathervane shows us that the wind can blow in four different directions.

The cards, numbered from one to ten, go through the development of a certain element from beginning to end. The court cards show us the rulers of a particular element— and in the day-to-day they are manifested in our relationships with others.

The cards of the Major Arcana are trump cards. They symbolize the higher knowledge, the spiritual knowledge that only a select few used to have access to. On a more mundane level, the Major Arcana indicate our attitude toward things to come, toward tasks that have been set to us. Many of us take certain things for granted—we are set in both our ways and our attitudes. However, there are those among us who are committed to self-development and to following a certain belief system stringently, however challenging this may prove to be. Perhaps these people are priests or hermits, but they may be found in many other walks of life as well.

There are 22 cards in the Major Arcana. Earlier on, it was mentioned that in a way a tarot card deck has 22 jokers—the whole of the Major Arcana. However, there is one card in particular that corresponds to the joker of a conventional pack of cards: the Fool.

In the following table, an ordinary tarot deck, a conventional pack of cards, and the Kalevala Tarot are compared.

THE MINOR ARCANA

TAROT CARDS	PLAYING CARDS	KALEVALA TAROT
SUITS		
Swords	Spades	Swords
Wands	Clubs	Stakes
Cups	Hearts	Dishes
Pentacles	Diamonds	Loaves
COURT CARDS		
Princess		Daughter
Prince	Jack	Son
Queen	Queen	Mistress
King	King	Master

THE MAJOR ARCANA

TAROT CARDS	PLAYING CARDS	KALEVALA TAROT
0. The Fool	The Joker	Lemminkäinen
1. The Magician		Ilmarinen
2. The Popess		Aino
3. The Empress		Louhi
4. The Emperor		Joukahainen
5. The Pope		Väinämöinen
6. The Lovers		Rakastavaiset
7. The Chariot		Isäntä
8. Force		Kyllikki
9. The Hermit		Vipunen
10. Wheel of Fortune		Taro
11. Justice		Äiti
12. The Hanged Man		Tiera
13. Death		Tuonela
14. Temperance		Ainikki
15. The Devil		Hiisi
16. The Falling Tower		Tammi
17. The Star		Marjatta
18. The Moon		Mielikki
19. The Sun		Poika, Son
20. Judgment		Ukko
21. The World		Luonnotar

THE KALEVALA

THE KALEVALA TELLS OF two warring peoples. The Kaleva people are the "goodies," and the Pohjola people are the "baddies." The Kaleva Heroes go on adventures to the Wild North. They encounter great obstacles and have many narrow escapes on the road to success, happiness, and riches.

The main Heroes are *Väinämöinen,* who was there before the world began, and who promised to return when times were better; *Ilmarinen,* who is Väinämöinen's traveling companion and who forged the heavens; and the spirited and passionate *Lemminkäinen* who seeks adventure.

Other Heroes are *Joukahainen,* who wishes he knew better than Väinämöinen; and *Kullervo,* who is the saddest of them all—constantly doing foolish things and getting himself and others into trouble.

Aino is a much-sought-after maiden who comes to a tragic end. She would rather go back to her childhood home than become Väinämöinen's wife. The wicked *Louhi,* mistress of the North, of Pohjola, has the Kaleva heroes pursuing her daughter and brings about the forging of the magic SAMPO. Following is a diagram showing how the Kalevala Tarot cards are arranged in accordance with the six main heroes around whom the Kalevala poems have been compiled.

Väinämöinen's Belt		The Major Arcana
Ilmarinen's Forge		The Court Cards
Kaukomieli's Blade	Fire	Wands or Stakes
Joukahainen's Bow	Air	Swords
The Fields of Pohjola	Earth	Loaves or Coins
The Kaleva Moors	Water	Cups or Dishes

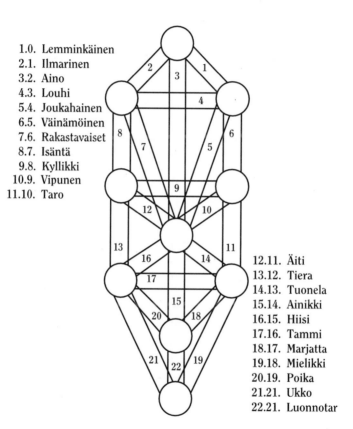

In the following is a diagram showing how the Kalevala tarot deck's Major Arcana accords with the Kabbala...

1.0. Lemminkäinen
2.1. Ilmarinen
3.2. Aino
4.3. Louhi
5.4. Joukahainen
6.5. Väinämöinen
7.6. Rakastavaiset
8.7. Isäntä
9.8. Kyllikki
10.9. Vipunen
11.10. Taro

12.11. Äiti
13.12. Tiera
14.13. Tuonela
15.14. Ainikki
16.15. Hiisi
17.16. Tammi
18.17. Marjatta
19.18. Mielikki
20.19. Poika
21.21. Ukko
22.21. Luonnotar

The Kalevala people in The Tree of Life...

THE KALEVALA FAMILY

| wife | Kullervo |
| daughter | son |

| mother | father |

| Marjatta | brother |

| mother | father |
| sister | Kalervo |

| wife | Untamo |
| daughter | son |

The Minor Arcana in The Tree of Life…

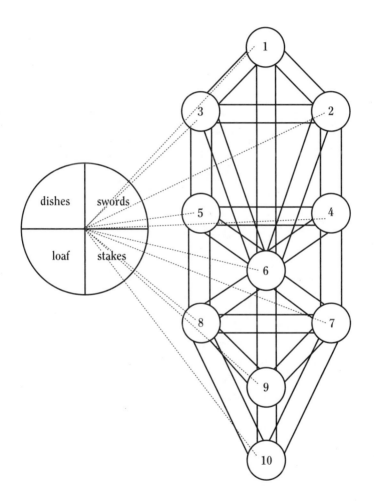

The Kaleva people in The Tree of Life...

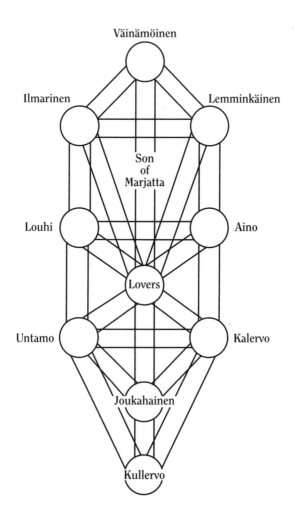

Six branches of The Tree of Life and The Kalevala...

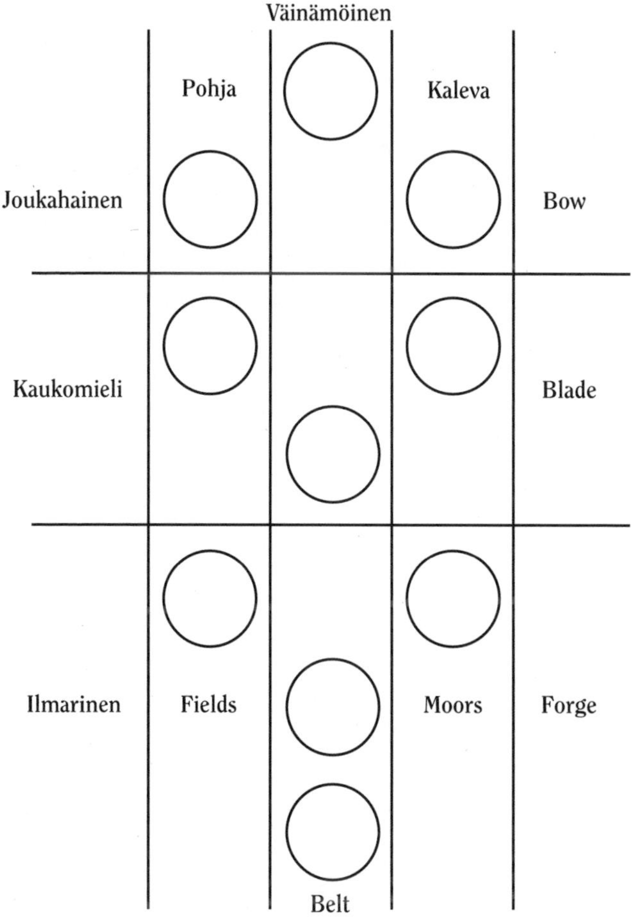

Väinämöinen

Pohja   Kaleva

Joukahainen   Bow

Kaukomieli   Blade

Ilmarinen   Fields   Moors   Forge

Belt

The Kaleva people in an Enneagram…

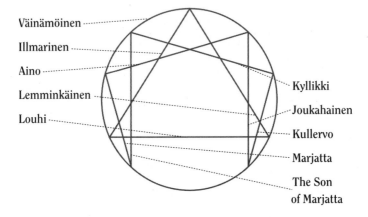

THE MAJOR ARCANA
VÄINÄMÖINEN'S BELT

VÄINÄMÖINEN IS THE CENTRAL figure of the Kalevala—he is involved, albeit at times indirectly, in most of what goes on there. Väinämöinen's belt symbolizes the eternal circle—another, more familiar, symbol of which is the snake devouring its own tail. Human spiritual development need never end; we can go round and round and deeper into the same themes, in an eternal circle.

The Major Arcana of the Kalevala Tarot corresponds to Väinämöinen's belt.

0. THE FOOL

Lemminkäinen

DESCRIPTION

Lemminkäinen is one of the Kalevala's main heroes. He is a wonderful singer—and a sweet-talker too. He can usually be found either in battle or seducing women. He seeks happiness, even ecstasy, in the pleasures of the moment; he lives according to his whims, whether they be angry ones or passionate ones.

THE KALEVALA

Lemminkäinen goes out into the world in search of a wife. He goes to The Island of Women. Before Lemminkäinen finds a woman he would like to wed he spends time enjoying himself with all the beautiful women on The Island. Then he woos Kyllikki, the most desired maiden of them all. Kyllikki will not have Lemminkäinen's hand. Lemminkäinen kidnaps her and takes her home.

Lemminkäinen promises to settle down if Kyllikki, in turn, will promise to give up the past pleasures of her youth. They swear an oath together, but Kyllikki breaks her oath and Lemminkäinen leaves home in anger. He goes to find new adventures and to fight new battles, leaving his mother, his wife, and his sister behind. Lemminkäinen goes to Pohjola and asks Louhi for her daughter's hand. Louhi sets Lemminkäinen to completing various tasks. On his third task, Lemminkäinen is killed by a cowherd and his body is cast into the Tuoni

River, from whence his mother comes to bring him back from the Dead. Lemminkäinen returns to Pohjola, where he slays the Son of the North. Lemminkäinen flees and eventually returns home, only to find that his home has been burned down by raiders from Pohjola. After many more escapades, Lemminkäinen joins Väinämöinen and Ilmarinen on their way to Pohjola to rob it of the Sampo.

PERSONALITY TYPE
A clown, a troubadour, an entertainer

DIVINITIES
Osiris, Alder, Zeus, Jupiter

SYMBOLIC MEANING
The sun and, in some tarot decks, the butterfly are symbols of hope and challenge. The dominant yellow color means that the Fool's life is ruled by abundant energy and by feelings. The white clothing symbolizes good intentions and a clear conscience. The orange showing underneath is a sign of vitality and sexuality.

The blue belt symbolizes Time. In the belt there are six pairs of triangles pointing toward each other—these are the twelve hours in a day. There are twelve months in a year, too—half of which are the summer months, the sunny months, and half of which are the wintry or dark months. You can only see one half of the belt; the other half is night and the stars we don't see, as they are behind the Earth.

There are five bells hanging from the belt; we have five senses with which to decipher our surroundings. The red headband shows that passion even reigns over Lemminkäinen's thoughts. The green hair means growth and creativity. The mountains symbolize challenges that have been faced and life that has been lived. They are green. The past has been good and brings hope into the present, even though the cliff the Fool is standing on is gray. Something is dulling it, and that is why he is looking up and out toward the future. The future doesn't exist, at least not yet—it is like the precipice the Fool stands at the edge of. The stick is symbolic of will, and the bundle is the knowledge and skills that have been sieved through experience and which aid Lemminkäinen on his journey through life.

The brown cape is like the everyday, which Lemminkäinen fills with color and with flowers. He is sunny, child-like and light-hearted. The lizard, which in some tarot cards is a dog either biting or snapping at the heels, symbolizes past neglects, failings, accusations, and duties, as well as memories and faithfulness.

ADVICE

You have arrived at a place in your life where the future seems threatening—yet there is no return. You now face the unknown. Your conscience hounds you, your past will follow wherever you go. You have come a long way—but what is the way forward? You don't really want to worry about that—you want to live a day at a time.

REVERSED MEANING*

Are you really living a day at a time—with the weight of the past so heavy on your shoulders? You wish you could change the past...well, you certainly can change the shape your future will take if you carry on in this same groove. You CAN! Start changing now. Tomorrow is too late.

The card is reversed when the Fool is upside down.

1. THE MAGICIAN

Ilmarinen

DESCRIPTION

Ilmarinen is one of the Kalevala's three main heroes. He is a good and trustworthy companion and helpmate. He works hard and is an excellent blacksmith. He is sensible, stable, honest and faithful. He exudes tranquillity. Ilmarinen is, at times, rather naive and a bit too eager too comply with the wishes of others. Ilmarinen has the tools with which to make and do many things.

THE KALEVALA

As often is the case with hard and conscientious workers, Ilmarinen does get abused by others, as well as rewarded. Of all the those who court the Pohjola maiden, he is the man who gains her hand in marriage. Ilmarinen is also Väinämöinen's faithful companion and right hand. Indeed, Väinämöinen depends on Ilmarinen's craftsmanship.

Väinämöinen promises Louhi, the Mistress of Pohjola, that he will bring her the Sampo. Väinämöinen manages to persuade Ilmarinen to go with him to Pohjola and there to forge the Sampo. After many trials and tribulations, Ilmarinen finally weds the Pohjola Daughter. However, Ilmarinen is soon widowed. He forges himself a wife of gold and silver, but isn't comforted. He woos the second daughter of Louhi, but his new wife so provokes him that he turns her into a seagull.

Väinämöinen and Ilmarinen then set off together for Pohjola to rob the Sampo.

PERSONALITY TYPE
A worker, a professional, an employer

DIVINITIES
Mercury, Hermes, Thot, Thor, Ilmaris

SYMBOLIC MEANING
One of Ilmarinen's hands points upwards, the other points down—according to Ancient Wisdom, what is up is also down. The positioning of Ilmarinen's hands symbolizes opposing forces. Sparks fly when they fuse, and Ilmarinen tames them and creates from them through utilizing another force, the force of his will. Ilmarinen is wearing a white tunic, indicative of his spiritual purity. His apron shows that his work in the world in no way tars or corrupts him—in fact, his work actually protects him and his spirituality. The red and blue on the collar of his tunic are, again, symbolic of the opposing forces interweaving in the Magician's work and life. The snake belt is symbolic of causality—beginning and end meet; as an old Finnish saying has it, "What you leave behind you, you find before you."

Ilmarinen's thick hair symbolizes his strength; his high forehead, his knowledge and intelligence. Over Ilmarinen's head is the symbol of Eternity—there is, after all, no end to the new thoughts and ideas that can be made real through work. The Magician has a strong physique—his spiritual side aligns with his worldly side, and he is a force to be reckoned with!

The hammer Ilmarinen is holding is symbolic of active will, of masculinity. The anvil is a sign of the opposing and equally powerful feminine force. Water symbolizes feelings; here it is in a cooling dish. Fire is symbolic of will and passion; Air feeds it and helps it grow. The treasures show the riches a job well done will bring forth, and the rocks show how a man is in the material world.

The green underfoot shows us the miracle of Creation—every spring the world renews itself and grows green again. There are nine treasures. This means that Ilmarinen rules over the mystical world of numbers.

ADVICE

The future can be formed by our actions in the here and now. You have come to a place where it seems that everything and anything is possible. You have all the tools you need for your task to be completed—what are you waiting for?

REVERSED MEANING

You find you have forgotten something. You don't have everything you need. You need all the parts in order to complete the Whole. Try and define what it is you need in order to carry on with your task.

2. THE POPESS

Aino

DESCRIPTION
Aino is an innocent maiden who lives in her own little world on the Kaleva moors. She is no longer a child, but not yet fully grown, standing on the threshold of womanhood. Aino is a hard-working and conscientious young girl whose fate others wish to decide. However, Aino just cannot bend her will to suit others. Aino's fate is symbolic of a man or woman giving up their dream and returning it to the collective consciousness.

THE KALEVALA
Joukahainen promises his sister Aino's hand in marriage to Väinämöinen, the old and steadfast. The brother and sister's mother rejoices, for Aino will have a well-known husband. But Aino weeps...Väinämöinen comes across Aino amongst some birch trees and makes advances. Aino flees. Mother tries to comfort Aino, telling her she should be happy and wear her best clothes. But Aino will not be comforted. She refuses to marry old Väinämöinen. She wanders off into the forest, where she gets lost. She comes to the seashore, sheds her clothes, walks into the sea and drowns.

Väinämöinen goes fishing for Aino. He catches a strange fish. He is just about to cut into it when it slips from his hand back into the water. The fish then speaks, telling him she is Aino. Väinämöinen fishes for her again, but in vain.

PERSONALITY TYPE
An innocent, a young girl, a virgin, a princess, a nun, a water nymph, a mermaid

DIVINITIES
Isis, Diana, The Moon Goddess, Artemis, Ilmatar

SYMBOLIC MEANING
Aino is sitting on a seat made of stone—this means you can only save your dreams if they have a strong foundation in reality. The stone in her lap is a symbol of ancient and eternal knowledge, of the Achasic records of time in which all that is known is written. In some tarot cards the maiden holds a book, the Torah or Pentateuch, which is the Holy Book of the Jews, just as the Bible is the Christian's Holy Book and the Koran is the Sacred Book of the Muslims. In this context, Aino symbolizes the Holy Ghost who can be reached by studying and living in accord with the Holy Writings. Round her neck Aino wears a gold chain. The chain, like the snake devouring its tail, is a symbol of Eternity. However, there is a Maltese cross on the chain, anchoring her in place and time. She is surrounded by water and air—these two elements place her in the world as well.

The trees on either side of Aino are opposites—the birch symbolizing femininity, and the pine, masculinity. There are two sides to Aino: she is of Eternity, is everywhere, and yet sits firmly on her seat waiting; whereas, for example, Lemminkäinen is standing still and yet is constantly on the move.

The moon in the water in front of Aino shows how Aino brings light to the world in much the same way as the moon reflects the sun. Her yellow hair, too, shows us that she is of light. On her head she bears a crown. She is a Goddess and rules the four main life principles. The fish on her crown shows that Aino dwells in the realm of the unconscious and is only a visitor in the material world. The colors of Aino's robe, blue and violet, are colors of nobility, sensitivity and refinement. Her surroundings are green and fertile, perfect as things are in a dream. The seven flowers show how Aino, like a flower, is ready to be plucked. She is ready—but unattainable.

ADVICE

For now, inactivity is most effectual. Things are happening in the dark, either in secret, or in our or someone else's thoughts. Once the thinking is clear, half the work is done. A lot happens behind the scenes and is only brought out into the light and shown to others much, much later. When this card is on the table, we need to be reminded of the importance of and wisdom in humble beginnings.

REVERSED MEANING

It is shallow to focus on superficialities. You are paying attention to trivialities. What is on the surface is not necessarily the truth—don't believe it is. You need to go deeper. Then you will touch the mystery.

3. THE EMPRESS

Louhi

DESCRIPTION

Louhi is the Empress of the North, of Pohjola. She reigns over the practicalities of everyday life. She knows what is needed and is also willing to pay the price to get it. Louhi and her daughter are well able to set the appropriate tasks for the different Kaleva Heroes. Louhi can be tender, but she can also be very stern, even extremely cruel, if her way of life, her property or possessions are being threatened.

THE KALEVALA

Louhi wants a talisman, a Sampo. Whoever forges it may have her daughter's hand. Väinämöinen persuades Ilmarinen to come with him to Pohjola. Ilmarinen forges the Sampo and the wedding is held.

The Sampo brings riches to Pohjola. Pohjola actually becomes wealthier than Kaleva. The Kaleva people become envious and this leads to war. In battle the Sampo is broken into fragments. Louhi curses the Kaleva land and hides the moon and the sun until finally Ilmarinen gets Louhi to release them.

PERSONALITY TYPE

A mother, Sophia, a mother-in-law, a lioness

DIVINITIES
Venus, Demeter, Kali

SYMBOLIC MEANING

Louhi is the ruler of property and possessions. She is mother Earth, the one who cares for the land and for what is hers. Louhi sits in front of the storehouse where tools, grain, and clothing are kept—all that we need as human beings to maintain and nourish us physically. The colors in the door of the storehouse form a distinctive pattern, showing us there is a place for everything, and everything is in its place. In a conventional deck of cards it is the diamond suit that symbolizes the material world.

On her head the Pohjola Mistress wears a cap, on which there are twelve stars. These are for the twelve months in a year and the twelve signs of the zodiac, over which Louhi rules. Hanging from each side of her cap are two looped ribbons, showing how the world moves—the Earth revolves round the sun, the position of the stars change, seasons change, years change. In Louhi's left ear she wears the sign of Venus; she rules over Aesthetics, over that which is beautiful.

The Earth's rotation and the changing seasons bring with it harvests and ripe fruit, such as the apples in the basket and the carrots on the bench. Louhi's masculine side is the side that protects and cares for her property—note the scepter in her left hand. However, the fact that it is in her left hand shows that her masculine side is the more passive side, springing into action when all else fails. In her right hand she holds three keys; keys to the past, present and future. Being the ruler of the twelve months, she holds Time in her hands.

The stripes on Louhi's dress show the different periods and different uses of time. In three of the stripes there are stalks of wheat, denoting love and responsibility. She wears blue socks, blue being the color for feelings—this shows that her emotions are in touch with the Earth, with nature. Hanging from her right ankle are two coins—Louhi is in active communication with others. The coins dangling from her left ankle denote gaiety, joy and happiness. Louhi rejoices in her communion with the concrete world. The hayfork on Louhi's left depicts her masculine and active need to reap a good harvest, to keep it in her storehouse, and share it, to the joy and happiness of all.

ADVICE

You must care for that which belongs to you; don't let anyone destroy it. Think carefully about how you can increase and maintain your material well-being. Take care of your friends and those that care for you. Make sure you don't avoid the more negative and difficult aspects of caring for what you own—everyone has a right to defend themselves and what is theirs.

REVERSED MEANING

You are giving away things that you should keep. It is your turn to receive and to take, yet you are being the giver and, thus, abusing others with your generosity and good intentions. Are you really going to soil your own nest? To allow your life to crumble and be destroyed? You are frittering away what you have worked for, and what is rightfully yours. There is nothing to stop you looking after it.

4. THE EMPEROR

Joukahainen

DESCRIPTION
Joukahainen is the first person to make use of acquired knowledge, of things already invented and created. In order to have access to these he must, first of all, conquer the original Creator, Väinämöinen. It all starts when he becomes envious of Väinämöinen because he knows more. Joukahainen wants to be the one who knows, the one in power—but Joukahainen's knowledge is always second-hand knowledge. He tries to overthrow Väinämöinen, but unsuccessfully.

THE KALEVALA
Joukahainen has heard about the great wizard Väinämöinen. He wants to be like him, to be better than him. He tries to outdo Väinämöinen, but is plunged into a swamp by him instead. He ends up pledging his sister Aino for his release. Joukahainen is embittered and becomes obsessed with seeking revenge on Väinämöinen. Joukahainen finally shoots the horse from under Väinämöinen, who falls into the water and swims to Pohjola.

PERSONALITY TYPE
A leader, a councilor, a manager, a consultant, a chief

DIVINITIES
Jupiter, Pluto, Lucifer, Hades, Hermes, Loki

SYMBOLIC MEANING

Joukahainen has grown older. He has learned, through many battles and experiences, to rule his empire. He sits on a throne which rose from the swamp he was sinking in as a youth. He is now a ruler of the elements. There are four ram's heads on the corners of the throne—these show the will that rules over the four elements—the same elements that Ilmarinen had on his table. They are also symbolic of the four aspects of a human being that very much decide his or her fate: good and bad, increasing and decreasing.

Joukahainen's silence and inactivity are by no means passive. He acts when it suits him to act. He wants to protect his abilities and his knowledge—hence the steel headdress he is wearing. Joukahainen really knows what he wants and makes this clear to others.

On the Emperor's head is a crown with three parts to it, for he rules over three worlds: the world of forms and concepts; the world in which he lives and acts, that is to say, his Empire; and his own nature and character, its leanings, its weaknesses, and its strengths.

Joukahainen's surroundings are rocky and bleak; nothing can grow in his world unaided by his will. His armor is made up of triangles and rectangles. This shows that he knows all he needs to know, and that everything is in place. All we can see of Joukahainen are his face and hands—he is shielding himself as much as possible, only baring what is necessary in order for him to be able to act. The blue on his sleeves shows that he does have depth and feelings, however hidden under the red cloak of deeds and action. The sky is red too—his world is constantly under threat—nobody or nothing better or more powerful than he may enter it. Joukahainen sits in the center of the picture— he is in the center of his own world and life.

ADVICE
You are the ruler of your own life. Regardless of your circumstances, fate has given you an important task—you must rule over what you have been given, the specter is in your hand.

REVERSED MEANING
The situation isn't in your control, but ruled by circumstances. Things are getting out of hand. Someone else has taken it upon themselves to control your fate. There is never time for a ruler to rest—s/he must keep a tight hold on the reins. Responsibility is a heavy burden.

5. THE POPE

Väinämöinen

DESCRIPTION

Väinämöinen knows everything. He knew of the world's beginning and was, indeed, instrumental in it coming about. In just about everything that takes place in the Kalevala, Väinämöinen plays a part—if only in that he gets others to do things on his behalf. Väinämöinen has great knowledge and great strength. At times these are his downfall, as he doesn't understand those weaker and less able than he, but expects them to be as capable as he is. His knowledge is ancient. Sometimes ancient knowledge can stand in the way of the new, and Väinämöinen isn't always able to make use of new skills. His difficulties in boat-building show how important it is that knowledge and skills are appropriate for the task at hand.

Väinämöinen finally finishes building his boat, but it doesn't bring him what he wanted, the Daughter of Pohjola's hand. His knowledge is a deeper, cosmic knowledge. Väinämöinen's fate shows how the old must, at times, give way to the new so that life can move on.

THE KALEVALA

Väinämöinen is tossed about in ocean at the beginning of Time until he finally lands on a treeless country. He sows trees, herbs, flowers, berries, and barley with the help of Pellervoinen. Väinämöinen is the Father of agriculture.

Väinämöinen competes with Joukahainen. He persuades Ilmarinen to go North with him and there to forge the Sampo. Väinämöinen would like a wife, but remains single. He is a rescuer, a wise man, a leader.

PERSONALITY TYPE
A priest, a teacher, an authority, a guru, a councilor

DIVINITIES
Odin, Zeus, Allah, Jahve

SYMBOLIC MEANING
Väinämöinen is playing a harp. Väinämöinen is himself an instrument; he brings with him knowledge from and of The Beyond and The Afterlife. He is a priest, a teacher and sorcerer, and others will learn from him, make use of him. Väinämöinen's listeners are Lemminkäinen and Ilmarinen. Lemminkäinen wants to learn from Väinämöinen how to go it alone; he wants to put Väinämöinen's knowledge to use in his own life. Ilmarinen, on the other hand, wants to learn how to use knowledge to serve others.

The hare listening to Väinämöinen wants to learn how to protect himself, how to escape from danger—he represents the human body. The squirrel represents the soul; he wants Väinämöinen's wisdom to nourish him. The swallow represents human spirituality and seeking new insights.

The pine trees behind Väinämöinen symbolize Ancient Knowledge—knowledge that has come with us from long ago and which now is complete.

Round Väinämöinen's neck is a pendant in the shape of Ukko's ax. Ukko's ax is the Finnish people's very own Tree of Life, on which Creation has been drawn. Väinämöinen sits with his legs crossed, showing that he has reached the summit of his own developmental curve. He sits sturdily on a stone, on solid ground. Väinämöinen's wisdom and knowledge are eternal and cosmic. The ferns represent the growth and hope that Väinämöinen's wisdom brings forth.

ADVICE

S/he who speaks of truth must take care to speak only of their own truth. You have a right to be honest with yourself and others and to speak to them—you do have a lot to say. Even if they don't agree with what you are saying, you can still ask others to listen. Your truth is as right to you as theirs is to them.

REVERSED MEANING

You don't have to be right. You might change your mind. Why not listen to someone else's truth—a strong person can see things from a different angle without losing their own perspective. Try to really listen to a friend, to really understand him or her, to see what they are getting at. Open yourself to new influences, experiment, do something unheard of, ask yourself more questions. Look to a new future once you have shed past burdens.

6. LOVERS

Rakastavaiset

DESCRIPTION

This card shows a situation where a person identifies with a member of the opposite sex. S/he becomes aware of him/herself by listening to, looking at, and touching another human being. This card is also symbolic of free will—we choose whom we want to identify with, project ourselves onto. It also shows that what can be joined together can also be brought asunder.

The card symbolizes the first point of contact, when a person becomes aware of another person's reality, of a world outside their own. In the Kalevala, two different ways of falling in love are described—their differences are both contained in this card.

ILMARINEN AND THE POHJOLA DAUGHTER

Ilmarinen, the smith, is assigned several tasks by Louhi. Aided by the advice of the Maiden of Pohjola, he plows a field of serpents; he also captures the Bear of Tuoni, the Wolf of Manala, and, finally, a large and terrible pike in the Tuoni River. Ilmarinen wins the Pohjola daughter's hand in marriage.

LEMMINKÄINEN AND KYLLIKKI

Kyllikki lives in the house of her wealthy father, from whence Lemminkäinen kidnaps her—he drags her to his sledge. Kyllikki weeps until Lemminkäinen promises to leave behind him the pleasures of youth, he will no longer go to war, just as long as Kyllikki no longer goes to the village dances. They will stay at home, be together and look after the homestead.

PERSONALITY TYPE
Lovers, husband and wife, companions, helpmates, couples

DIVINITIES
Amor, Agape

SYMBOLIC MEANING
The card shows two people embracing. They are committed to each other. Behind the man there is a bonfire—it is the traditional Finnish Midsummer bonfire, the "Juhannuskokko." Behind the woman are birch trees and water. Man and Woman unite. Opposites unite—water and fire unite. Nature is at its most beautiful. Everything is in flower. The bee flies to the apple-blossom. The sun is shining.

The angel above blesses the young couple. Promises are being made which will change both of their lives.

This is the card of love and commitment. The lovers either decide to go their own ways, or to leave the past behind and build a new future together. After this nothing will be the same. On the left of the couple is a road—the road to their future.

This card can also indicate that a decision needs to be made, perhaps to do with work, education, or anything else involving a big commitment. An important choice has to be made and, once made, there will be no looking back. Of course we all know that failing to choose is also a choice.

ADVICE
You have a choice—either you can go your own way and stay free and independent, or you can share your life, your hopes, your dreams with someone else. This is where opposites meet

and things which might have seemed unlikely, or well nigh impossible earlier on, are now a reality. What once seemed desirable no longer does. However, you still have to choose— take it or leave it.

REVERSED MEANING
It is so hard to choose. Both alternatives seem just as good. You waver. As soon as you lean in one direction, the other direction seems more tempting, and vice versa. There is nothing for it— you must make your mind up, for better or for worse.

7. THE CHARIOT

Isäntä

DESCRIPTION

The Master of Pohjola is a doer—he is both conscientious and decisive. He keeps a tight rein on all things and is very goal-oriented.

THE KALEVALA

Lemminkäinen and Isäntä don't see eye to eye. Lemminkäinen demands bread and ale and is given them. However, he refuses to eat and drink in the doorway of the cottage at Pohjola, but wants to be invited in. He goes in, sits himself down and demands better ale. The ale is still fermenting and the Mistress of Pohjola and Lemminkäinen quarrel. Isäntä challenges Lemminkäinen to a duel, in the course of which Lemminkäinen strikes off Isäntä's head.

DIVINITIES

The seven stars of the chariot:

SATURN — The environment is more influential than the inner life.

JUPITER — The inner life is more influential than the environment.

MARS — The individual is at the height of her/his powers and very unpredictable.

The SUN — The universe revolves round the individual.

VENUS — The individual's vitality is more important than the circumstances.

MERCURY — The individual is trying to learn and to develop.

The MOON — The individual projects him/herself onto the environment.

SYMBOLIC MEANING

Isäntä sits in a chariot which represents his achievements and the structure of his life. Often, in particular in dreams, a house represents a person's life—here the chariot performs a similar function. The chariot has four pillars—one each for North, South, West and East. The driver of the chariot is balanced and at peace with his feelings, thoughts, strengths, and his reality.

On the roof are painted the seven constellations of the chariot. Isäntä is aware of these seven influences on us—of vital power, sexuality, emotions, love, sight, awareness, and communication. On top of the roof is a streamer indicating nobility and spirituality.

The forest he is driving through is deep and dark—his life is full, there is much to accomplish both materially and spiritually. The road is bumpy and hard. Everything unnecessary, anything luxurious, has been discarded—Isäntä moves forward on with just the ground under him. The stones underneath appear to have an order to them, the road has been paved before Isäntä—he is no pioneer, he follows a given route.

The wheels of the chariot are the wheels of fortune. Isäntä is at the mercy of fortune—all he can do is go forward with faith. The heads on either side of the chariot symbolize the victory of will—it has cut short its never-ending dialogue with reason! One of the heads is for rational thought, the other for intuitive thought. They both submit to Isäntä's will. Two bears pull the chariot, symbolic of the polarities good and bad, both pulling in different directions. Still, the driver holds the reins firmly. On these are rune signs—symbols of both ancient and new knowledge. With the help of these the polarities are steered and the chariot can move forward and eventually reach its goal.

Only the driver's head and hands are bare, showing his humanity and willingness to reveal himself. Other than that he is well-protected. His credentials are good and he has no doubts about the importance of his mission. He can do nothing else but go forward.

Isäntä wears a crown with four horns, on which there is a moon. This shows that he has control over his life, his fate, but that the dark side to him still dwells in the world of imaginings and superstition.

The sun on his front shows that he wants to be at the center of things—he wants the world to rotate round him. The world *is* turning, regardless of Isäntä—it ensnares him, and he believes he is indispensable.

ADVICE

You have come to a decision, you have chosen. What more do you need? You need your parting orders and to be shown to the door and out onto the road. The forces within you are pulling in different directions—look ahead and keep a tight hold of the reins.

REVERSED MEANING

You are drained, your strength has been misused and now you are frightened. No matter how hard you try, nothing seems to happen. Are you really going to let a good opportunity pass you by just because of a squabble? Squabbling and brooding won't get you anywhere.

8. FORCE

Kyllikki

DESCRIPTION

Kyllikki of the Island is a strong-willed and decisive woman. She has very definite opinions and she wants to keep her independence, married or not. She is a woman who wants to have a home and a husband, and to care for these, but also to have a life outside her four home walls. She wants to be both a free woman and a wife. She is self-sufficient and is on good terms with her wild side, her free side, her dream side. She is spontaneous, following her whims of the moment. Kyllikki comes from a wealthy family and is wooed by many. She lives a happy and free life with the other maidens of the Island. She is the most beautiful and strong-willed maiden of them all. She turns her suitors down, and even though Lemminkäinen finally forces her to come with him, she still retains her independent spirit.

THE KALEVALA

Kyllikki comes from a good home. She has many, many suitors—they come to woo her from far and near. She wants none of them and is happy with her friends, the other women of the Island. Then Lemminkäinen comes along and kidnaps her. They finally come to an agreement about how their life together will work, but after a while Kyllikki gets bored and misses her carefree life with her friends. She goes to meet them. Lemminkäinen is furious and leaves home for new adventures.

PERSONALITY TYPE
A feminist, a career-woman, an egalitarian, a companion

DIVINITIES
Athena, Freyja, Europe, Helena, Hera

SYMBOLIC MEANING
This card is about how individuals use their power.

In a wintry landscape, a scantily dressed maiden opens the mouth of a wolf with both hands. The wolf is symbolic of vitality, of brute force. Kyllikki's dress is orange, showing her sexual power. This card shows three forces, or rather, one force at work on different levels. There is, first of all, the force of the will to survive, the force that makes flowers bloom and the grass grow. It is blind, explosive, and even seems horrifyingly cruel at times. Then, there is the sexual level, shown in the colors of Kyllikki's hair and dress. This is for the perpetuation of the race—it is a magnetic force.

Last of all, there is the spiritual force of Kyllikki, of the woman herself. In this context the word *energy* has a very specific meaning—energy comes into being through Kyllikki using and channeling these forces, in much the same way as the power of rapids can be harnessed for electricity. The world around Kyllikki is covered in snow—it is a cold place. The maiden is in a rigid and bleak reality—an ungiving world where energy is and must be used sparingly.

The birch and the pine tree show the polarities at work, the increasing and decreasing energies, the Yin and the Yang, as do the shifting blues and turquoises in the snow. The Aurora Borealis in the sky is yet another symbol of the force at work; it needs to reflect from something or show up in contrast with something else to be seen. Again, the changes from light to dark show that force is a process, increasing and decreasing constantly.

Behind the maiden and the wolf are three shadows. Force is perceived differently at different times. The shadows represent the past, present and the future. They also represent our fears—the forces are seen from different perspectives depending on where we are spiritually, too.

Kyllikki has tamed her power—the shadows exist, but they are behind her and their heads are turned away from her. They have no power over her—Kyllikki has claimed her own power and tamed it with understanding, patience and love. There is no violence in Kyllikki's expression—she meets her opponents with tenderness even though she won't give in to them.

ADVICE

If you want to keep your freedom and independence, then the first person you need to have on your side is YOU. You need to be patient with yourself, with your fears and your anger. Otherwise these will find their way into the world outside you and do damage. When you love yourself, love and friendliness will be channeled into your being in the world.

REVERSED MEANING

You are rushing things. You are anxious. Your fears have got the upper hand and your judgment is being affected by them. Nothing is going where you want it to, and the smallest of obstacles seem enormous. Slow down. Try and concentrate. Try to be patient, most of all, with yourself.

9. THE HERMIT

Vipunen

DESCRIPTION
Vipunen is a giant with immense knowledge who lies in the bowels of the earth. It is said that he, in his great hunger, swallows people. He represents the past and is the ruler of past knowledge. He is the Earth's memory.

THE KALEVALA
Vipunen was a great giant who lay, as if he were dead, under the earth. He had taken knowledge with him. Trees grew on him. Väinämöinen felled these and forced open Vipunen's mouth. The giant woke from a deep sleep and ended up swallowing Väinämöinen, who then caused him stomach pains until Vipunen gave him the magic words he needed to finish his boat. When Väinämöinen left Vipunen's body he had heard how the sun, moon and stars were born, how the earth was formed from water and how plants first grew on it. He had also learned countless spells and charms.

PERSONALITY TYPE
A wizard or wise person, a historian, a psychiatrist or psychologist, a therapist, a doctor, a scientist, a thinker

DIVINITIES
Dionysus, Bacchus, Balder, Ahriman

SYMBOLIC MEANING

In many cultures and religions, knowledge is described as being like a tree. A person, too, can be seen as the tree which the seeds of knowledge nourish and help to grow. We learn from ourselves, from others and from our surroundings. Jesus speaks of sowing—some seeds fall in good and some in barren soil—the soil, here, being human beings.

There are nine trees in this particular card. Just as all other numbers are derived from the numbers 0-9, in humans there is all we need to learn, all we don't yet know.

It is night—this shows a being hiding inside his awareness, his inner growth, the fruits of his subconscious. He no longer looks to the outside, but the trees show that he is still growing. The owl, too, is symbolic of wisdom.

The being in the picture has his eyes open and can see what is going on around him, but no longer participates in it. The lakes on each side of him are symbolic of feelings—they are calm. There is life elsewhere—there are mountains behind one of the lakes—but the giant is indifferent to it. The Aurora Borealis shows knowledge reflected against the heavens, that is, spiritual knowledge, divine knowledge. It is the knowledge the super-ego possesses and only becomes visible at night, in silence when a person is on his or her own. The leafy trees are symbolic of knowledge dependent on time, knowledge that will serve for a certain period and then will be dated. The evergreens are symbolic of permanent and timeless knowledge.

ADVICE

If you really want to learn, then you must look deep inside yourself. Only you can know what is best for you. You have got to go on a spiritual journey—the road ahead might be difficult, but never as difficult as your fears and imaginings would have you believe. You are walking in the dark—go at a steady pace and one step at a time.

REVERSED MEANING

You will always be lost if you look for the answers elsewhere. Do you really think someone out there knows better than you do what is right for you? Only you know what is best for you—and, although there is nothing wrong with listening to good advice, only you can lead yourself out of the confusion you are in.

10. THE WHEEL OF FORTUNE

Taro

DESCRIPTION

In the Finnish language fate is *kohtalo*—take away the first syllable and you are left with *talo*, meaning *house*. A house is a place, a home—and our fates are the place we're in. The word for womb, *kohtu*, is another such word—the womb is our very first place, the place in which we grew in order to get to this place. Astrologers define this place by studying where the stars are and have been placed on certain significant occasions in an individual's life.

THE KALEVALA

Fate is a mystery which decides our lives for us—yet fate can also be the summation of our actions. Fate is the place where an individual finds him/herself at a certain point in time. The deeds we do all contribute to our fates—the things we leave undone means we leave part of our fates behind. Time brings a new dimension to fate—it brings with it new things, but also brings back the old. Fate is where we are at a certain time—and how we got there, that is to say, where we were at all the points of time along the way. The Wheel of Fortune turns and spins further on the threads that run through our lives. Fate is the place, the time, the way, the action and the surviving. Fate is the spanner in the works.

PERSONALITY TYPE
A gambler, a career person, a student, ratrace, a competitor

DIVINITIES
Moirat, Nornat, Wyrd

SYMBOLIC MEANING
The Wheel of Fortune turns and, when it stops, we are given something. Yet, our fates are something we ponder over and try to imagine—our fates are shaped partly by our thoughts and our dreams. These must, of course, be put into action with much determination and will-power. Fate determines our lives. It is like the Elk of Hiisi that Lemminkäinen pursues—his doing so decides his moves, his whereabouts and his thoughts. It is also like a bear, who with one sudden stroke of his paw can completely change a life.

Väinämöinen, the old wise one, believes he should rule over fate—and he is, indeed, one of the movers of the Wheel of Fortune. However, the eagle is far more powerful than he—the eagle can carry a person off as easily as if s/he were a hare. Here we can see both how great and how insignificant Man is. The squirrels show how often Man goes round in circles, powerless and getting nowhere. It is only awareness that brings him any power to determine his fate in the slightest.

Another interesting Finnish word in this context is *taro*. *Taro* is a neighborhood or a village, a *taromaa* is cultivated land. It also means that there is enough of something—*taro* of something. For example, one could say that something was *taroisa* and that would mean that it contained something significant, something meant to happen. However, being *tarossa* means being in trouble!

ADVICE
Fate is playing with you. There will be a change for the good or the bad soon. It is good to take whatever comes philosophically and to remember that actions still can matter.

REVERSED MEANING
The Wheel of Fortune is spinning you round, and you are trying to hang on to things already behind you. You long for safety and for what you knew, but must now face the new and all your insecurities. For all you know, once you feel safe, the new might well turn out to be better than the old.

11. JUSTICE

Äiti

DESCRIPTION

Lemminkäinen's mother ("Äiti" in Finnish) is a caring one—she tries in every possible way to protect her son. The world is a cold and treacherous place. Äiti finds it hard to believe that her children will manage out there unprotected. Äiti's lap is the safest place, the best place. Caring is key to Äiti's being. She never judges her children when they fail, but understands that circumstances were against them—in fact she usually knew that from the start, but she also knows her children must try their wings whether it worries her to distraction or not.

THE KALEVALA

Äiti tries unsuccessfully to persuade her son Lemminkäinen not to leave home. Later he does return home, bringing a wife with him. Äiti accepts her son's choice of spouse. Lemminkäinen goes off on his adventures again and Äiti fears for her son's safety. She goes to look for him. After much searching she finds the fragments of her boy's body and brings him to life again, using charms and magic salves.

Äiti bids Lemminkäinen to seek refuge on the Island of Women, where his father once lived in peace during a year of terrible war. Here Lemminkäinen is happy till the menfolk return. He then sets off on adventures, yet again, and these result in his house being burned down. Lemminkäinen weeps for his mother, believing her to be dead. But to his great joy, he finds her alive and safe in the forest.

PERSONALITY TYPE
A judge, a policeman or -woman, a nurse, a healer, a repairer

DIVINITIES
Gaia, a Madonna, Astarte, Isis

SYMBOLIC MEANING
This card depicts life between two worlds. Äiti is standing between two trees—a birch tree and a pine tree. These trees aren't necessarily opposites—it is just that if you have to choose between them they become opposites, as that which is good in the one, is bad in the other, and vice versa. As such, these opposites attract. They are like night and day. Daytime is consciousness, where all is beautiful, such as the butterfly on Äiti's shoulder. Night is subconsciousness where we only have a moonbeam to guide us. The sun is shining brightly, awareness is complete, whereas we only see a tiny sliver of the moon. The rat on Äiti's shoulder shows how repulsive we find the mysterious workings of the subconscious. The antlers on Justice's head show that she lives in both worlds, in the night world as much as in the day world.

When a person thinks holistically, s/he has a foot in both worlds and acknowledges her or his dark side as much as the conscious side. S/he doesn't try and reason this side away, but doesn't let it take over, either. Otherwise, what happens is that things eventually become so unbalanced that difficulties arise.

The children at Äiti's feet are also symbolic of the struggle for balance between these two worlds—they struggle, pulling each other back and forward, and neither child wins or loses. Äiti is on her toes, as she is partly of the air. This position, too, indicates the importance of maintaining a balance in our lives and environments.

ADVICE
Justice is in giving as well as receiving, in donating as well as taking. You have a verbal side, which is ruled by reason in the form of concepts. You also have an emotional, intuitive side which is ruled by pleasurable feelings. It is good to have these sides in balance and working together. Try to be aware of which side is more prominent in you and to give the other side of you more room the next time you make a choice or a decision.

REVERSED MEANING
Things are out of kilter. They aren't in balance. You have been giving one aspect of your life too much attention. Which one is it, reason or feeling, that is getting the upper hand? Do you have too much knowledge, yet not enough skills—or vice versa? Are you doing too much and thinking too little, or aren't you doing enough, are you analyzing every detail, your every move? Try and establish where it is that you are not in balance.

12. THE HANGED MAN

Tiera

DESCRIPTION

Tiera was Lemminkäinen's companion. Lemminkäinen and he came from similar backgrounds—they both had strong mothers and strong ties with their homes. Tiera was impressionable and could easily be led astray. Tiera's and Lemminkäinen's relationship was similar to Väinämöinen's and Ilmarinen's—where one is very much the leader and the other follows. Tiera agrees to join Lemminkäinen in an expedition to Pohjola, but after several unhappy events, Tiera decides that the life of travel and adventure is not for him. He decides to till land and be a family man instead.

THE KALEVALA

Tiera joins Lemminkäinen on an expedition to Pohjola. Tiera's parents don't want him to go—they try to stop him by reminding him of his duties and his young fiancee. Louhi sends the frost against them and it nearly is their undoing, but Lemminkäinen uses his powerful charms to combat it. Tiera eventually gets lost. He makes his way home and resolves to stay there.

PERSONALITY TYPE

A worker, a manager, a page, a farmer, a farm hand, a civil servant

DIVINITIES
Odin, Osiris, Shiva, Achilles, Gilgamesh

SYMBOLIC MEANING
A man is hanging from a tree branch upside down, by one leg only. His other leg is bent. He looks satisfied—he is even smiling. This is certainly a position it would be hard, indeed well nigh impossible, to be in—and, in particular, to stay in in real life. Still, the man in the picture seems happy enough! It seems likely that he could free himself if he wanted to—after all, his foot is tied to the branch with a very simple and loose knot. Obviously, he'd have to work at it; it wouldn't necessarily be easy. However, it doesn't look as if he's trying to get free—it seems he hangs there willingly.

The fact that the man is hanging head downwards means that he approaches things from a different angle and therefore sees them in a different way. He seems happy—his happiness is no longer dependent on his surroundings, but on his attitude and way of seeing.

The man is surrounded by a bright yellow light. This means that he is at peace with himself and his fate, that happiness shines brightly on him regardless of the fact that frightening or negative things are going on—note the four skulls on stakes on the left. The skulls are symbolic of old laws, which perhaps no longer have any meaning, but sometimes need to be taken into consideration anyway. The swallows show how the hanging man's thoughts and dreams are free to fly in the sky of imagination, where they can cheer the bleakest of situations and give an illusion of freedom.

The man's trousers are red, which shows that his passion and joie de vivre are as strong as ever. His belt is blue—his emotional side isn't repressed, either. His feelings are, however, changeable, as can be seen by the golden pattern on the belt. The fir tree on the right symbolizes the insight this man has—

he hasn't forgotten what he knows and what he can do, he uses his knowledge even as he is hanging.

ADVICE

The present moment is at the crossroads of place and time. How you relate to this moment is a matter of choice—the circumstances are what they are, only your attitude to them can change. Seize the moment, seize the day, carpe diem! Nothing may change—apart from you. Our lives are lived moment by moment—live these moments truly.

REVERSED MEANING

Time passes. Circumstances change. One thing leads to another. But, you are living in the past or for the future. You never seize the moment. Don't let life pass you by—it is the present that is real. Be aware of your abilities and potential. Grab the chances you have, now, to build the future with them.

13. DEATH

Tuonela

DESCRIPTION

In the Kalevala, the river of Tuonela is the place where you are taken after death. It flows between life and death. The bad get banished to the river. It is where the deceased make amends for their deeds. It is where one wants the people that one hates or is burdened by to go. Sorcerers and shamans can go there from the land of the living in the shape of animals, or when in a state of trance.

In ordinary life we all visit Tuonela in a way—we all have times of depression, times when we feel humiliated and defeated, when all we once believed in and hoped for now seems meaningless. Tuonela is where all our disappointments go. We do come back from Tuonela—but only after we've had time to mourn and to pull ourselves together.

THE KALEVALA

Lemminkäinen goes to shoot the Tuonela swan. The cowherd Märkähattu lays in wait for Lemminkäinen and wounds him with a water serpent. Lemminkäinen, thinking he is dying too young, misses the wise council of his mother. Märkähattu pushes Lemminkäinen into the river and hews him into fragments with his sword.

PERSONALITY TYPE
Sick, convalescing, depressed, imprisoned

DIVINITIES
The River Styx, Valhalla, Ghede, Seth

SYMBOLIC MEANING
The blackness, the bleakness, show the landscape of depression. However, there are four flowerbuds growing in the stony ground. There will be new life, the buds are waiting for better and lighter times—so there is hope.

Lemminkäinen is in fragments in the river—a depressed person is as if in pieces. The river is dark and merciless self-pity—it has no pity on those who wallow in it. The snake threading its way through the fragments of Lemminkäinen shows the treachery of pride and self-centeredness and how they poison and kill. The legs of the skeleton are broken—they are symbolic of shattered illusions. Illusions never were real—therefore it isn't circumstances, or reality, that have thrown the person into depression. The depression is of his or her own doing—s/he brought it upon her/himself, was in the trance of believing the illusory. When these illusions reveal themselves as what they are, a person's image of their own uniqueness and importance is shattered. The bow and arrows show the person in question's willingness to fight and defend him- or herself. S/he was defeated and is down.

ADVICE
Your failures, your shattered illusions, can give birth to new life—if you would only let go of your selfishness, your ego's need to shine. Once that happens, there will be many surprises. You need to become stronger in order to accept what has happened. Yesterday is dead. You can't carry on in the same way—the new, the present has its own way. You will start

spinning the web of the future with the new insight and new ideas sprung forth from your time in Tuonela.

REVERSED MEANING

The seed of success is germinating in the future. Look to new things. Time and work change where you are in life. Start planning your new life—there is no going back. Try to keep an open mind, even if you seem to be stuck and unable to act on anything. In time the changes will happen. Time is like the phoenix that rises out of its own ashes. Time is reborn in the next moment, and the next, and the next...

14. TEMPERANCE

Ainikki

DESCRIPTION
Ainikki can't control things, but she can intervene. She believes her motives are the right ones—she is only trying to help "a little" with a few words here and a few gestures there. Of course, these few words might change the whole nature of things. Ainikki moves things on, moves them forward. Selfishness and unselfishness alternate, just as the negative and the positive do.

THE KALEVALA
Ainikki is Ilmarinen's sister. She was doing the washing early one morning when she saw Väinämöinen on his way to Pohjola to woo the Pohjola Daughter. When Ainikki found this out she told Ilmarinen about it. Lemminkäinen also had a sister whose name was Ainikki. She was the one who told on Kyllikki when Kyllikki went off to the village to meet her friends. Because of this, Lemminkäinen went off—and both Lemminkäinen's and Kyllikki's promises to each other were broken.

PERSONALITY TYPE
A well-wisher, a spiteful person, a secretary, a public relations person, a diplomat, an assistant

DIVINITIES
Aphrodite, Demeter, Mary Magdalen

SYMBOLIC MEANING

Ainikki is the maiden of the dawn and the twilight—of the in-betweens where opposites meet. She doesn't belong to either one or the other, but stands one foot on the firm ground of Permanence and one foot in the flowing river of Time. She is pouring milk from a silver container into a gold one—she can change the negative into positive and vice versa. She can alter points of view and ways of seeing things. Few things are good or bad but thinking makes them so. In many other tarot decks, the woman pours from the gold into the silver.

The sun shines beyond the horizon, it is either rising or setting, the day is ending or beginning. This is the time of preparation for the next stage. This is the card of rites of passage, where we let go of the old and prepare for the new. The violet fells stand between Heaven and Earth—violet is the color of enlightenment. With awareness and understanding we can join opposites, or at least know where they belong and where they can meet. The grass is green. Things are growing all around Ainikki. The lilies are in flower by the river.

Everything we do gives rise to something. The smoke rising from the cottage shows it is lived in, it is being heated or food is cooking. The trees are newly in leaf—we can get an inkling of what is to come. Preparation is the beginning of change.

Ainikki is only half dressed. Half of her skirt is orange and the other half is indigo blue—in the colors of her skirt we see the balancing of opposing elements. Ainikki involves herself in things and has influence, yet part of her remains hidden. She wears three chains round her neck for the three stages in creativity— the thesis, antithesis and the synthesis of it—the force, the opposing force and, finally, their harmony. On the chains is a pendant with a figure showing the movement a swinging pendulum makes. Time is measured in the toing and froing of a pendulum.

Ainikki is wearing a headband with an ornament on it. This lies on her forehead. She has a third eye, with which she can see the potential in opposing forces, the new dimensions they can bring into sight. Ainikki seems at peace with herself. By joining opposites, by not denying the one or the other, we can find harmony. Ainikki has light sandals on her feet—she is with us and at the same time she is not—she is able to be separate and yet still remain involved.

ADVICE
Things sometimes occur which won't necessarily affect you—or at least it is hard to see how they would. They still matter. Perhaps you will be able to turn the bad into good. You are standing with one foot in the river of Time and one foot on the riverbank. You are standing in Time and Place and the moment meets you—will you accept what it brings to you with open arms, or with a grimace? Only you can decide and perpetuate your attitude. The power you have in all this is neither good or bad— it is what you make of it. This is so every minute of your life— these minutes are all we have.

REVERSED MEANING
You have been centered on yourself too much, you've had no idea about what is going on around you and this can be important, too. Remember that you can't always judge a book by its cover— there could be bad in what seems to be a good thing, and good in the bad. Life is passing you by—the moments are passing you by and life is in them. After all, the past has already happened and the future hasn't. You are living in these, yet life is happening now. Notice the moment. Stop and look at life. Good ideas need good plans behind them. In order to plan, you need to know where you are—now. The river of Time flows, and it can't be fast-forwarded or rewound.

15. THE DEVIL

Hiisi

DESCRIPTION

Hiisi was once a place where sacrifices were made. It was a far away, ominous place where the Ghost of the Mountain lived. In the Kalevala there was the Elk and the Horse of Hiisi. There was also the evil spirit of the forest—Metsähiisi. Hiisi was also an isolated and frightening person or giant. Nowadays, Hiisi is the same as the Christian's devil.

THE KALEVALA

A great wedding feast is held at Pohjola, lasting several days. An enormous ox is slaughtered for it. The tail of the ox was in the south of Finland, while the head was in the north. It took a swallow a day to fly from horn to horn. And the moon didn't get from head to tail in a month. When the ox was transported to Pohjola, it took a hundred men to hold its horns and a thousand to hold his muzzle. The ox was so big it was hard to find the right man to butcher it. They searched for the man both far and wide. They searched in Estonia, in Sweden, in Karelia, in Russia and in several other places. They even looked in Manala for such a man as could butcher the mighty ox—but found no one.

One day a dark man rose from the sea. He was iron-fisted, wore a helmet and had shoes of stone. He held a gold-bladed knife overlaid with copper. The butcher for the ox had been found. The ox yielded a hundred barrels of meat, a hundred fathoms of sausage and seven boat-loads of blood for the wedding guests.

PERSONALITY TYPE
A jealous person, a drunkard, a drug addict, a symbiotic relationship or a person enslaved by passion

DIVINITIES
Mithras, Dionysus, the Satyrs, Bacchus

SYMBOLIC MEANING
In the picture are three figures—an ox with a human torso, and two humans with horns and tails. These three symbolize the three lower states of Man.

The ox is symbolic of Man's material and physical needs. He stands on a brown rectangle, showing how Man has given his life to serving these needs and worshipping the pleasures they bring. In so doing, he has made the ox into a torch-bearer, a great challenge and reason for living.

There are two humans—Man and Woman. Man and Woman unite and become one in the sexual act. The man carries a torch, like the ox's torch, on his tail—his passions and physical needs rule him.

The woman, in turn, worships fertility as well as pleasure, hence the apples on her tail. She worships the cup in the hand of the ox—it gives the greatest pleasure of all. Both humans are imprisoned in the material. They need concrete goals and pleasures in order to act. The horns are symbolic of pleasure and reason—the horns don't meet. The man's raised hand shows he is ambitious—he wants much material gain. The woman only sees immediate pleasures and needs. If the appetite cannot be satisfied, there is no hope. All else is in the dark, is unknown.

ADVICE
You are imprisoned in the material. Pleasures and things are holding you down. They are seducing you. They rule your actions. Habits, too, can make you stuck, can tie you to things.

REVERSED MEANING
Your indecisiveness is taking all your strength, draining you. In order to move forward, you need to make a decision now. Otherwise you will be left behind.

You need to change your habits and routines for your circumstances to change.

16. THE FALLING TOWER

Tammi

DESCRIPTION
The oak is a mighty World standing over creativity and growth. All strength is being used on just surviving. Molehills are becoming mountains, hiding all that is happening.

THE KALEVALA
Pellervoinen scatters seeds in the bare earth. Trees and swamps were born. Plants soon cover the earth. However, Väinämöinen notices that there is no oak tree. At first he cannot get the oak to grow. Turso, a beast from the sea, burns all growth and plants an acorn in the ashes. The oak grows and grows. All else is in the shadow of it and never sees the sun or moon. Väinämöinen looks for a man who could fell the oak. Väinämöinen prays that Luonnotar, Mother Earth, would send powers from the ocean to fell the tree.

From the sea emerges a man, small of stature, who says he would fell the mighty oak. Väinämöinen finds this hard to believe. In three blows the man fells the tree.

PERSONALITY TYPE
An agitator, a terrorist, an anarchist, a zealot

DIVINITIES
Shiva, Lucifer, Mars, Loki, Ares, Seth

SYMBOLIC MEANING

The oak depicts a person's beliefs and attitudes. These have become so big that they stand in the way of new knowledge entering his mind.

In the picture it is winter. A person living by reason and logic alone seems cold and devoid of feeling. The feelings are there, however, as the sky is orange. It is just that reason has all the power and is not letting feeling through.

Man is small and, at times, he makes insignificant things, things born from unconscious needs and fears, loom so large that they threaten to stifle and overshadow everything he has worked for and built. Anxiety, the black cloud, brings forth a thought, the eagle, that can spoil the best of plans.

There are two people falling from the oak-tree, a man and a woman—they have been living in an ivory tower, indeed. Now they will have to start all over again. They can no longer live the sheltered lives they used to, but, naked as they are, have to face the cold world outside. They are now unencumbered and ready to see things in a new way, and no longer in the shadow of old values and convictions. They can live fully again, once the thing that loomed so large and important in their lives has been struck down.

ADVICE

Something you believe in is being put to question. Perhaps your mind has been playing tricks on you? A small thing changes everything and the truth is suddenly revealed. Now it is time to break the chains that habit has bound you in and make your way into the new, just the way a butterfly emerges from a chrysalis.

Old ways and habits, old choices and reasons no longer make any sense.

REVERSED MEANING

Don't resist what you have found out so suddenly. What was good and true yesterday no longer is so. Things change, they grow old and wither, they grow out of and into; they transform. It is time to let go. Don't fight the changes—nothing ever stays the same. The way forward is through acceptance.

17. THE STAR

Marjatta

DESCRIPTION

Marjatta was a stranger, an outsider even in her community.

People were cold to her and she knew what it was to be unsupported and unprotected. She did have a happy childhood, but after she became pregnant, and thus flouted convention, she had to fend for herself. However, regardless of her own needs, she continues to work for the common good.

THE KALEVALA

Marjatta was happy in her childhood home for longer than usual—she certainly wasn't in a hurry to get married. She was self-sufficient and also very particular about her dress, her food and what she did. She once refused to milk a cow just because it had been among the bulls. When her father asked her to go sledging she would not sit in a sledge drawn by a stallion—or even by a mare who had been with a stallion.

Marjatta goes to the hills to watch over the sheep, but life as a shepherdess doesn't suit her either, and Marjatta is easily distracted from her duties. She swallows a cranberry and this makes her pregnant.

PERSONALITY TYPE

A religious fundamentalist, a critic

DIVINITIES
Mother Earth, Mother Nature, The Virgin Mary, Isis, Astarte, Ishtar, Esther

SYMBOLIC MEANING
The naked woman stands with one foot in the water, and one on the ground. She is standing with a foot in both worlds—in the world of the subconscious, of the emotions and spirituality, and in the concrete world, the practical, everyday world, the world of rationality and logic. Marjatta is pouring water into the lake—this symbolizes her giving of herself, of her wisdom and understanding to the Cosmic Consciousness. She is pouring milk onto the ground, showing how she nurtures the material world, too. In this world there grows a tree, in the branches of which twinkle the stars of the Great Bear. The pole star is the star highest up against the sky.

This card shows that this woman is exceptionally giving—she gives of herself to others. Her good deeds spread rays of light where there was darkness. Where once all was bleak, there is now good cheer. Where once it was barren and stagnant, there now is growth and flow. Marjatta is naked, for she has surrendered herself wholeheartedly to the universe, to God. She has become a part of nature.

The stars in the Great Bear all seem to be pursuing the pole star. This signifies what happens when differences are no longer in competition, but work together. Many little things, little deeds add up and can become something mighty.

The seven stars all signify slightly different activities—contracting, expanding, conquering, disappearing, merging, adapting, and changing. All these activities are focused on the one pole star; forces have united to reach a common goal.

The pole star is symbolic of the meaning of the woman's life, and of her faith—she has a star to guide her. The pole star is her goal and the seven other stars are like goal posts, or signs pointing her in the right direction and strengthening her faith. She will get there a step, a star, at a time. Old Finnish sayings have it that the Great Bear portrays Lemminkäinen hunting the Elk of Hiisi. However, the woman in the picture won't get to her goal by one great act of derring-do.

It will be the cumulative effect of the activities in her daily routine that get her where she wants to be. She will, perhaps, study, she will work hard, and her feelings about her studies and work will make her every day a day of celebration. She will take nothing for herself, but pour herself into everything. However, she won't confuse things. She won't expect what she does to be praised or even noticed. The way she sees it, everything has a purpose and everyone has their part to play in it.

ADVICE

Dreams give birth to fancies which, in turn, can spark off wishes. Wishes can become targets, can become goals. From things that have happened, from your thoughts and your day- and nightdreams, a vision has emerged. A guiding star is on the horizon of your life. Maybe you will never reach this star, but you will be following it from now on.

REVERSED MEANING

Treat your passing fancies as arrows, as pointers, rather than as anything that you definitely have to give in to. Think very carefully before you take action. Sometimes dreams aren't meant to come true; sometimes the price for that is too high. Your dream might be there to teach you, and to give your life renewed meaning.

18. THE MOON

Mielikki

DESCRIPTION
Mielikki was capricious. When in a good mood she would yield excellent prey, but on a bad day she would just taunt you. She was the mistress of the forest. Sacrifices were offered and prayers said to her, for on her belt were the keys with which to let loose the hunt for the hunters. As mistress of the forest, Mielikki kept dogs, wolves and other beasts. Sometimes she lost people, cattle and pets in the forest and they could only find their way out with the help of the right spells and incantations.

Mielikki made a bear from wool that she took from the water where the moon had cast it. She nurtured the bear under a pine tree. Before she gave him teeth and claws she made him swear an oath not to do any mischief with them.

FATE
Lemminkäinen was set the task of capturing the elk of Hiisi. The task proved to be a difficult one, so he turned to the deities of the forest for help. First he turned to Ukko, the highest of Gods, for snowshoes with which better to chase the elk. Then he sang to the hills and the pathways and trees of the forest and asked Tapio, the master of the forest, and his son, Nyyrikki, to guide him safely to the quarry. Finally he praised Mielikki. He pleaded and prayed to her not to taunt him, but to yield him the elk.

PERSONALITY TYPE

A public relations or advertising person, an agent, a manager, a graphic designer

DIVINITIES

Artemis, Circe, Diana, Hecate, a Valkyrie

SYMBOLIC MEANING

Mielikki herself isn't shown in the picture, but she is certainly present. She reaches others by taking on different forms. The pond symbolizes emotions and the subconscious; the pond can mirror these. The shell with a pearl in it shows how the good may be protected. However, in a narrow, sheltered life cut off from outside influences and dangers, the good is less likely to be seen or put to use. The grass or reeds around the pond show a potential for growth and usefulness. This person's life is about practical results.

The wolf signifies the bestial side of Man, the intuitive side. It is a frightening side for most of us. We fear the unfamiliar, what we sense will happen and yet cannot explain why rationally. We fear the Mystery, and yet want to touch it at one and the same time. This is why we watch horror movies and read tales of vampires—for the wolf inside us all.

The fox—clever, cunning and quick—stands for slyness. He often gets what he wants, but seldom in a straightforward way—more often he uses tricks and manipulation. People delude themselves, they rationalize, they often seem to not know what they are doing when it is obvious to everyone else! At times their conflicting desires can lead to them seeming to be oblivious to a side of themselves which is wreaking havoc, hence the saying, "the left hand doesn't know what the right hand is doing."

Treachery, lies and deceit have played a significant role in many faiths. Yet cunning wasn't necessarily always used for the bad; at times it was used as the only possible means to a good end. Zeus often used his cunning to get humans to act. Odin changed shape in order to seduce women. The Indian ape god Hanuman came to the aid of good forces with his cunning and quickness. However, Loki caused great confusion with his lies—so much so that he was called "the father of all liars"! For the North American Indians, a coyote represented mischief, cunning and destructive forces. A coyote, a fox, and a hare still often represent these attributes in the cartoons of the modern world.

The cliffs to the left and right show how narrow the insight and perception of one human being are. S/he has built his or her own structures on them woven into the pine trees. There is method in her or his beliefs! The moon in the background shows there is a goal s/he is aiming for. The stars are other elements in the person's life that, albeit important, don't hold a central position. They cast a light, but the moon's light is central and much stronger.

The path leading from the pond through the cliffs represents the path a person chooses in life. Perhaps the path was only chosen after much deep thought; but paths are often made while reaching for the moon, or because of nostalgia, a passing whim or temptation.

ADVICE

You are living in a world of dreams, hard for your conscious mind to grasp; everything seems unreal. Memories and associations surface from your subconscious. You are trying to understand this world with your intellect and to weigh things up in accordance with your principles. Your imagination is being stretched. There is no way, at the moment, that you can make any decisions based on what is going on inside your head.

REVERSED MEANING

Beware now of making choices and decisions. Try to avoid arguments and disagreements, as well. Things aren't what they seem and you might get them wrong. Don't jump to any conclusions. It is so easy to believe that what you imagine to be, really is. Wait and see…

19. THE SUN

Poika, Son

DESCRIPTION

The boy came into being under very strange circumstances. He brought with him new possibilities, as he couldn't in any way fit into the old molds.

We humans often reject and try to cast off the new and the unfamiliar. We don't easily let a stranger into our midst. We discriminate against someone or something "different." But Poika wouldn't just go away. He stood up for his rights and therefore the path was opened to new beginnings.

THE KALEVALA

Marjatta's boy had no father—a cranberry Marjatta ate impregnated her. Everyone rejected Poika except for his own mother. One day Poika left Marjatta's lap and went off into the woods. Marjatta set off to look for him. She asked a star, the moon, and the sun if they had seen him. The sun told Marjatta that the boy was in a swamp. Marjatta found him and brought him back home, with great rejoicing.

The boy needed a name, but Virokannas wouldn't agree to baptize the fatherless boy until Väinämöinen had advised him to do so. Väinämöinen sentenced the boy to death, but the child himself reproached him for the unjust sentence. The boy was then baptized as King of Karelia and the Lord of all the mighty.

PERSONALITY TYPE
An innovator, an inventor, a reformer, a man or woman of ideas

DIVINITIES
Christ, Apollo, Horus, Vesta

SYMBOLIC MEANING
A child is skipping, naked, among the flowers. Two birds, one a dove and the other a brown grouse, are flying above him. The sun is shining brightly in a cloudless blue sky. In the background is a brown fell. A child symbolizes renewed enthusiasm and rebirth. He is naked; completely open to life and living to the full.

The birds stand for ideas, for new thoughts and insights that make life in this world all the more worthwhile. The brown bird shows how ideas can be prey for some, that they can be abused. The child still skips in blissful ignorance—he is just happy to be alive and has not yet a care in this world. The flowers show how all the new is just waiting to be fertilized—or to be plucked. The fell is for all the challenges and responsibilities that are yet to be taken on, and for rules and laws to be followed in the process.

The midday sunlight illuminates everything—there are no shadows or secrets. This is a moment of truth, where everything is fully visible.

The child's hands are lifted and open toward the heavens. He is ready to give himself to higher and greater things, and receptive to warmth and love. He is as innocent and untouched as the flowers in the field—he has not yet been wounded. The dove is flying toward his outstretched hand, showing the child's receptiveness; and the grouse flies away, showing his givingness.

Together, the boy and the birds symbolize the receiving and passing on of all good things. The child keeps nothing for himself, because he has more than enough. He doesn't need to save things, to store them, but he passes them on. Hence, he is free to dance in the warm sunlight and wonder at the world. He is a new arrival in paradise—he has no answers, he wears no clothes, but is open to life and loves it with all his being.

ADVICE
Everything is possible, once again. A new dawn brings with it new possibilities. The smallest and, seemingly, most trivial of things just might save the whole situation. Don't be shy—make use of the new openings. The new must be appreciated. It has a right to be here.

REVERSED MEANING
Look the facts in the eye and accept them. Stop daydreaming! Start working toward your goal, even if all you can do now is very little—the seeds of the new are nearly always small.

20. JUDGMENT

Ukko

DESCRIPTION
Many belief-systems have a supreme God—often this God is the God of the winds and the weather. Ukko is the supreme God of old Finnish folklore. He lives high in the heavens, from where he rules the clouds. People pray to him for rain and for help in war, in sickness and when hunting. The other gods, too, are under his rule.

THE KALEVALA
Marjatta's son was to be baptized. He was brought before Ukko. Ukko refused to give the boy a name, because the boy was fatherless. The boy was brought before Väinämöinen, who told him to go back where he came from. However, the boy then spoke up for himself. He mentioned Väinämöinen's own crimes, as they had not been judged so harshly.

PERSONALITY TYPE
A judge, a critic, an inspector

DIVINITIES
Jehovah, Jumala, Vishnu, Indra, Zeus, Jupiter, Tor, God

SYMBOLIC MEANING
An old man is flying with the help of his purple cape. Around his neck he wears a pendant, made of gold and shaped like an ancient ax. He holds one of his hands over the people, as if to

restrain something in them. A finger of the other hand is pointing at one certain person. The sky is bright and colorful—indeed, all the colors of the rainbow can be seen in it. There are some white clouds on the horizon.

The people, men, women, young and old alike are naked and listening to the judgment. One of them is rising up out of her coffin and the others are rising up out of the swamp. There are three fetuses in the swamp—signifying future potential and possibilities. Eight spermatozoa swim in the ground.

This card depicts the whole of Creation. Things surface from the depths—some of them old and familiar, and others new and developing. This is how the different aspects of a personality can be seen. We are constantly trying out and taking on new roles, different ways of behaving and expressing ourselves, showing different personae and drawing from different archetypes. This same is shown, too, in the sky, in which we can behold all the colors of the spectrum.

The wise old man represents the spiritual side of Man and Womankind, and judges these different aspects and roles and ways of behaving. He has power, he is in a position to judge, as symbolized by the gold pendant he wears. His purple cloak, however, symbolizes his spirituality—he is able to judge these people wisely.

With one of his fingers he indicates that his attention is focused on one particular person, and with his hand he holds the others back—just as when we are with other people we often concentrate on one particular aspect or role at the expense of other sides to ourselves. The people in the picture are naked—what we see of them is real and they have nothing to hide. The criticism and condemnation comes from themselves, from that higher self or super-ego who sees through our other aspects. Even when the criticism comes from the mouth of someone else, it is still our inner judge that takes it on board and gives it validity.

The fetuses and the spermatozoa represent the constant evolution of our many different points of view. We are constantly testing new experiences, insights and ideas, and these change us in one way or another.

Every problem is faced and every solution found while we flounder in a place that is neither completely of our emotions and sub-conscious, nor is it completely rational and practical. The swamp symbolizes this place—it is both of water and land.

Indeed, life first stirred in the primordial swamp and not on terra firma. Later it became more varied, taking on new forms while some of the original forms, no longer best suited to the ever-evolving world around them, died out. These prototypes went back into Mother Nature's lap, from whence they were born, yet again, in different forms.

The Kalevala Tarot cards are well fitted to being used as an aid to making assessments and correct judgments. Every card depicts an aspect of a person's personality or their spiritual development. The person consulting them is like Ukko looking at the people in the picture, only now s/he is looking at the different people inside her or his own head. S/he and only s/he can be the judge of what is right for him or her.

ADVICE

You have to be able to decide what is wrong and what is right for you—just in the same way as you have decided to put things either to one side or to take them with you, when clearing a path for yourself. What is it you want to clear out of your life? And what do you want to develop and work on?

REVERSED MEANING

The mess you've gotten yourself into is now feeling very uncomfortable. You can get yourself out of it and enhance your quality of life. Use your own judgment to do so. What do YOU think would be the best thing to do? You have a right to thoughts and opinions, especially regarding your own life.

21. THE WORLD

Luonnotar

DESCRIPTION

All primitive religions have spirits ruling over the natural world, spirits who brought this world into being. Luonnotar is of the earth, and everything will eventually return to her. There are three Luonnotars, or Daughters of Creation, in the Kalevala. They were the mothers of iron; indeed, iron originated and flowed from their breasts all over land and water. In the very center of the earth, under the Tree of Life, there is a fountain beside which the Luonnotars reside.

THE KALEVALA

The Virgin of the Air descended into the sea, where she was impregnated by the winds and the waves and became the Water-Mother. A teal built its nest on her knee and laid its eggs. The eggs fell from the nest and broke. The fragments of these eggs formed the earth, sky, sun, moon and clouds. In time, these forms will return to the Virgin of the Air's lap until she, once again, descends into the sea.

PERSONALITY TYPE

A wife, a mother, a daughter, a maiden, a step-mother, a daughter-in-law

DIVINITIES
The Virgin Mary, Isis, Rauni

SYMBOLIC MEANING
In the card Luonnotar is dancing, naked. She is encircled by a snake devouring its own tail. A transparent veil is woven round her. She is holding a hammer in one hand, and in the other she holds a curved stake. Above her is the white of an egg, and she stands on the yolk. In each corner of the card there is a tree, symbolizing the different points of the compass.

The snake's skin has runes on it—showing how knowledge has become organized. They also depict time as a journey that starts and ends in the same place, just as the hands on a watch do. Inside the circle is a space, a space in time—a place. A human-being is born in a time and a place. Through his or her birth the great mysteries of life, birth and death are, once more, expressed. All this is present in the symbolism of the picture.

The four trees symbolize air, water, earth and fire. These elements are in everything: in humans, in animals, plants, rocks and the earth itself. They are in all the manifestations and forms of Mother Nature.

All that exists must be received and accepted—hence Luonnotar's nudity. She is innocent. She dances her creative dance inside the snake—the inside and outside of which separate good from evil. Luonnotar is naked, open, and yet protected. From her springs forth everything that is, for better and for worse, and to her it eventually returns. She brings about growth, but also death. She builds, but also lets things disintegrate and recycle. Nature belongs to every living creature and all may have their share of her.

The trees also symbolize the Kalevala Tarot families. They represent the future, standing for growth and new processes. The pine stands for the stakes, the rowan tree for loaves, the birch for dishes and the spruce for swords.

The whole creative process from start to finish is shown in the card. Everything returns to its beginning. The individual dissolves and merges with the universe, only to become differentiated once more.

ADVICE
The work has been done well. You have achieved what you set out to do. The road has been a long one, but now that you are here you can see that it was worth every step you took. For the moment you can enjoy what you have built and created—you have brought things forth and made them into being. After that you should think of what you want to do next. It will soon be time to sow the seeds for new beginnings.

REVERSED MEANING
You are nearly there, on your last lap, but your strength is waning. You are longing to move on to new things and leave others to complete the present task. However, your future hinges on completing this yourself. Leaving the task half-finished will make for difficulties later on—you will be burdened by the unfinished business—whereas completing it will give you a good foundation and lead to openings in the future.

HUMAN (SOCIAL) RELATIONSHIPS

LOAVES	STAKES	DISHES	SWORDS
MASTER father	leader	male relative	chief
MISTRESS mother	forewoman	female relative	officer
SON brother	active companion	male friend	partnership
DAUGHTER sister	passive companion	female friend	advisor
REALM home	work	neighborhood	business relationships

THE COURT CARDS
ILMARINEN'S FORGE

ACCORDING TO THE KALEVALA, poems were found under Ilmarinen's forge. Ilmarinen's forge was the place where the smith heated the iron in order to shape it into different things. A person's job, fate, age, social position, and influence can be likened to a forge for spiritual development. The court cards of the Kalevala Tarot represent Ilmarinen's forge. Ilmarinen was the second to main character in the Kalevala. He was Väinämöinen's companion and helpmate in all difficult tasks. The court cards are most useful with regards to relationships—either in such a way that the card describes the actual relationship, or one of the people in it.

THE SWORD FAMILY

THE PRINCESS OF SWORDS
Kullervo's daughter, an advisor

Thinking, reading and acquiring knowledge. Learning about and pondering over things of the spirit. Clarifying things. Curiosity about and interest in trivia, too.
Issue: Being aware of thought processes.

REVERSED MEANING
Suspicions, doubts, hints, whispers, unexpected messages—all causing alarm and giving rise to disagreements.
Issue: Resisting thinking.

THE PRINCE OF SWORDS
Kullervo, a partner

Thinking to some purpose. A good observer. Someone who wants to clarify things in order to move on. There is a goal, the achievement of which requires a great deal of concentration. You might need to read up on or find out about something.
Issue: Learning to think.

REVERSED MEANING
Deceit, espionage, falseness, secret activities, any goings on where the aim is to get information in an underhanded way. Thoughtless talk, empty words.
Issue: Not thinking, denying the importance of clear thinking.

THE QUEEN OF SWORDS
Kullervo's mother, an official

Intelligence and institutionalized knowledge. The preservation of systems and traditions. This person wants to climb the career ladder using his or her own skills and knowledge. The knowledge s/he has is valid. Beware, you of little faith!
Issue: The preservation of skills and knowledge.

REVERSED MEANING
An untrustworthy official, someone whose knowledge is dated, is trying to maintain their position. Competitors are kept away by gossiping about them.
Issue: Confusion.

THE KING OF SWORDS
Kullervo's father, a chief

Authority. This individual knows their stuff. They are worth listening to. It is, however, very hard to influence them in any way. They believe their word is law, that they know all there is to know—and won't even consider anything new.

Issue: The use of skills and knowledge.

REVERSED MEANING

Indecisiveness and insecurity. This person listens to others, tries to please them and never gets a word in edgewise. S/he might be very principled, but believes others know better and, therefore, gives in to them.

Issue: The abuse of skills and knowledge.

THE STAKE FAMILY

THE PRINCESS OF STAKES
Kalervo's sister, a passive companion

A powerful and decisive person whose goalposts are constantly shifting. Someone who takes on challenges unreservedly. A person who wavers when halfway there, who changes her or his mind. Someone unpredictable and restless, who springs surprises on others.
Issue: Becoming aware of one's will.

REVERSED MEANING
Someone who picks fights because of their restlessness and insecurity. Someone who hides their impatience and turns their energy inward, resulting in depression and inactivity.
Issue: Resisting one's will.

THE PRINCE OF STAKES
Kalervo, an active companion

A good-natured person with a lot of enthusiasm and spontaneity. Someone who seizes an opportunity, but also someone who goes into things head first. It is important for them to use more judgment and to get their priorities straight.
Issue: Knowing your own will.

REVERSED MEANING
A selfish, careless, quarrelsome, bossy and domineering individual. By being argumentative and blaming others, they try and rid themselves of their own bad feelings. Winning becomes more important to them than the principles involved.
Issue: Rejecting your own will.

THE QUEEN OF STAKES
Kalervo's mother, a forewoman

This individual enjoys power and wealth. S/he is an independent person who wants to work according to their own timetable and rules. Where there is a will there is a way for her or him. Despite his/her competitive streak, s/he is very warm and friendly, although extremely fierce when threatened!
Issue: The use of power.

REVERSED MEANING
A lazy person who should get their act together, but who would rather have others run around for them—they feel that the others owe it to them!
Issue: The crumbling of power.

THE KING OF STAKES
Kalervo's father, a leader

This person has got what s/he wanted. Someone with a strong will and a lot of determination. Getting results, reaching goals, fulfilling ambitions. Self-confidence and self-assuredness. Courage, but not foolhardiness.

Issue: Strong determination.

REVERSED MEANING
Selfish, demanding and manipulative behavior. Lack of self-confidence leads to abusive and violent behavior when all else fails.

Issue: Insecurity.

THE DISH FAMILY

THE PRINCESS OF DISHES
Marjatta, a female friend

Quicksilver. Someone trying to come to terms with his or her own feelings. This is a person whose good intentions often backfire, who often does themselves more harm than good, as her/his emotions are still ruled by the ego.
Issue: Being aware of one's own feelings.

REVERSED MEANING
This person is denying what is most important to them—their feelings. They push anything good or happy away, in order to protect themselves from hurt and disappointment. Strong and pent-up desires are seeking an outlet.
Issue: Denial of feelings.

THE PRINCE OF DISHES
Marjatta's brother, a male friend

This person is trying to get in touch with their own feelings. Good things are as much a part of life as bad things are. Everyone deserves their share of the good—and much can be learned from it. Feelings aren't articulated, but they are very much there. There is a readiness to consider for others, too.
Issue: Learning about feelings.

REVERSED MEANING
Rejection of anything happy or pleasurable. Dreams are pushed under. Sorrows and worries have taken over. Depression. Surfacing feelings are being repressed. The person is trying to escape from them into the cold world of reason.
Issue: Rejection of feelings.

THE QUEEN OF DISHES
Marjatta's mother, a relative

The ability to create a good atmosphere and good cheer. Romance and candlelight. This person is at their best when arranging a party. S/he is a good listener and easily gets very involved in other people's problems, sometimes too much so. *Issue:* Protecting one's own feelings.

REVERSED MEANING
An irritated, bitter or bored person. Someone who is fed up to the teeth of hearing about others' problems. They just can't listen any more, they have enough problems of their own. They might speak ill of those they have listened to for too long. *Issue:* The encouragement of bad feelings.

THE KING OF DISHES
Marjatta's father, a relative

This person enjoys life to the fullest. Sensual pleasures mean a lot to her or him, and s/he goes from one to the next. It is most important for them to feel good in luxurious surroundings.
Issue: Living for feeling and pleasure.

REVERSED MEANING
Shirking responsibility, because it doesn't feel good. The hard facts are being evaded, because *they* don't feel good. The individual themselves ends up feeling very bad, not good. There is a tendency, perhaps, toward alcoholism.
Issue: Penting up negative emotions.

THE LOAF FAMILY

THE PRINCESS OF LOAVES
Untamo's daughter, Sister

Routine. Acceptance of the everyday, of the things that become tedious, but still have to be done. Badly paid or voluntary work.
Issue: Acquainting oneself with the everyday.

REVERSED MEANING
A passive resistance to things that should be done—hence you procrastinate and nothing does get done. There are obstacles, real or imagined. Perhaps there are a few small practicalities that need attention before you can get down to the real task at hand.
Issue: Resisting the everyday.

THE PRINCE OF LOAVES
Untamo's son, Brother

Learning about practicalities. Apprenticeship. Hard or demanding work. Work given to others because you aren't able to do it yourself. Work in which it is well worth paying for other's expertise.
Issue: Learning about the everyday.

REVERSED MEANING
Escape into helplessness. Hiding behind not knowing how to do something—even though it would be easy to learn, you still aren't prepared to make the effort. Powerlessness.
Issue: Rejecting the everyday.

THE QUEEN OF LOAVES
Untamo's wife, Mother

Maintaining and caring for what you own. A generous and caring person for whom caring for the environment and for what they have is a priority. This person holds the roof up. S/he keeps everything in shipshape condition. S/he does try to keep others under control because s/he sees the well-being of the group or community as being of paramount importance.
Issue: Caring for what you have.

REVERSED MEANING
A selfish and avaricious person, someone who just wants more and more. S/he is inclined to envy and sees others as always being out to use them.
Issue: Neglecting what you have.

THE KING OF LOAVES
Untamo, Master

Acquisition of possessions or wealth. A trustworthy person—one who keeps his or her word and who knows their stuff. A professional person, an expert in their particular field. Someone very determined and single-minded.
Issue: Taking care of what you have.

REVERSED MEANING
A materialist. Someone obstinate or inflexible and, thus, very resistant to change. This person has no time for beauty or the arts—the hard facts are all that count.
Issue: Squandering what you have.

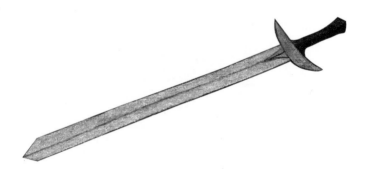

THE MINOR ARCANA
JOUKAHAINEN'S BOW

According to the Kalevala, poems sprang forth from Joukahainen's bow. Joukahainen's bow is the crossbow with which Joukahainen shot at Väinämöinen.

One person tries to influence another with words. At times these words are intended to hurt or to gain control over someone. Obviously, words that are well-timed and thought through will have the best and noblest effect. Such words can turn the bad into good; such words can heal. Joukahainen was an inexperienced and power-hungry youth. His aim was to overthrow the powers-that-were.

In the tarot, Joukahainen's bow corresponds to swords and to the element of air.

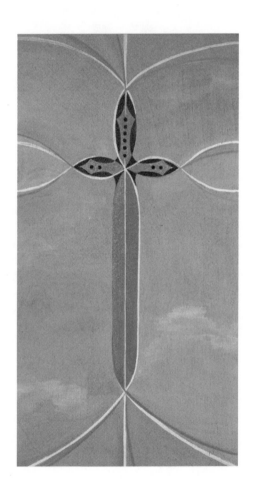

JOUKAHAINEN'S BOW

A struggle comes about because of differences. Air signifies the struggle between two people, using words as weapons, over concepts and space. Perhaps they have grown in a different direction, perhaps their circumstances used to be similar, but now no longer are. Streams of air coming from different directions meet, vibrate, mix and then find new paths. In the Kalevala Tarot, the symbol for this process is the sword. When different concepts and different visions meet, a struggle ensues.

Issue: A struggle is about to begin.

Advice: The seeds of empowerment and success are in your possession. You need to sow them, nourish them and let them take root. You are just about to succeed. However, you fear the worst and are worried, anxious, and depressed. You are the one who can change your own life for the better. Think of all the good things you could make your tomorrow be and set yourself some goals.

REVERSED MEANING

Things are only just beginning to take shape, they aren't yet complete. Don't jump the gun. You need to be clear about things before it is sensible to proceed. Things are swimming inside your head. Rest assured—you will find the way you wish to go, but you do need to go carefully and slowly at first.

Issue: Going slowly now will save time in the future.

Advice: Tread softly now. Go forward slowly and steadily, a step at a time. Haste could spoil things for you. Check your plans for flaws. Revising and perfecting your plans now will save you time in the long run.

TWO OF SWORDS

The adventurous and aggressive Lemminkäinen met the free and independent Kyllikki. They swore an oath to leave the ways of their youth behind them and settle down. They were married. It is good to face things without prejudice and weigh them up before coming to any value judgments about them. Things are what they are. Perhaps you can make some compromises and come to an agreement about things.

Issue: Things are equally balanced—you stand a fifty-fifty chance of getting what you want.

Advice: You just don't seem to be finding any solutions to your problems. Should you do this? Or that? Everything seems equally right or wrong. You need to try a different approach. At the moment, your feelings alone are deciding for you.

REVERSED MEANING

You are writing something off before you have even explored it properly. You are jumping to conclusions and forming opinions about things you know nothing of. Perhaps what you are thinking about isn't even the real issue in question.

Issue: A hasty decision.

Advice: Usually, you can come to decisions based on the circumstances. Sometimes, though, things can change so quickly that any decisions worth making are out of the question and you just have to let things happen.

THREE OF SWORDS

Aino's mother grieved for her. She cried three rivers over her daughter. From the rivers there rose three rocks, on which there grew three birch trees. Three golden cuckoo birds cuckooed on the branches of these. Human beings are all very different. Not one single one of us can completely share another's fate. We are all separate, and at times that saddens us. Sharing, intimacy and union with another are but momentary things.

Issue: Partings, disappointments and sorrow.

Advice: In order to get what you want, you need to sever the bonds that are holding you down and getting in your way. It is painful to let go of the past, sometimes it feels unbearable to do so. You are grieving. You will be going through a time of arguments, quarrels, and disputes with your nearest and dearest.

REVERSED MEANING

Petty squabbles might lead to a big row and a break-up with someone. At first all your little differences with this person seemed insignificant—but they were the prelude to the inevitable parting of your ways.

Issue: Different perceptions take you and someone else in different directions.

Advice: You are going through a time of confusion, sorrow, tears and despair. You feel desolate and long to be comforted. Things are in flux. Think before you speak, as arguments over trivialities may eventually cause a major break-up. Somebody needs to say they are sorry.

FOUR OF SWORDS

Joukahainen shoots Väinämöinen's horse. Väinämöinen falls into the water and drifts for eight days. On the ninth night he realizes that he no longer has nails on his toes or joints in his fingers, as they have been soaked off in the water. He laments his fate. An eagle finally carries him off to Pohjola.

Issue: There is no reason to hurry.

Advice: Leave things well enough alone. Talking about them and brooding over them will just make matters worse. It is very hard to remain objective. Do, however, try to think about other things; let your dreams, your subconscious, do the problem-solving.

REVERSED MEANING

Don't skirt around the problem from the outside. This time it can't be solved that way. You need to be inside the problem to come up with a solution. Do, however, still beware of making hasty decisions, as circumstances are changing all the time.

Issue: You must take an active part in events.

Advice: Try to get a grip on things, a little at a time, if need be. You might feel that you have no strength at all, but the smallest move is better than nothing at this point. After that you can think about the next step at leisure.

FIVE OF SWORDS

Joukahainen challenges Väinämöinen to compete over who is the wiser. When Joukahainen realizes that he isn't doing as well as Väinämöinen, he takes to his sword. Väinämöinen is enraged and forces Joukahainen into a swamp.

When fighting duels, there are two things to remember: first of all you need a contender; second, sooner or later you will meet a contender more powerful than you are. The choices your contender then makes will decide your fate.

Issue: Facing up to facts.

Advice: Look around you. You are too fixated on yourself and your own goals. If people aren't given the chance to contribute, they leave. You are being thoughtless. Using force might bring about results—but these will have no support behind them and might just as well be the trappings on a stage set.

REVERSED MEANING

If your attitude doesn't change, the results will be marred. Your obstinacy isn't doing you any favors, and you are getting in so deep that sooner or later it will be hard to extricate yourself.

Issue: Being obstinate will just make things worse.

Advice: Don't let your pride get the better of you. Do try and broaden your outlook, so that there is room for others in your vision. Perhaps you have been dishonest, but find that making things good would be very complicated. How about trying a different approach and seeing how far that gets you? Do be careful, though.

SIX OF SWORDS

Väinämöinen asks Ilmarinen to come to Pohjola to forge the Sampo. Ilmarinen refuses to go. So Väinämöinen persuades Ilmarinen to climb a wonderful pine tree. He causes a whirlwind to carry this tree straight to Pohjola. Once there, Louhi offers Ilmarinen her daughter's hand in marriage if he forges the Sampo for them.

Once the goal is set, you mustn't let anything stop you.

Issue: Go for it!

Advice: You are going through a difficult stage at the moment. Look to the future. Think of what it could be like. Life cannot but go forward, so do and say what is necessary for it to do so in the happiest possible way. Only take with you what is absolutely necessary. Heavy burdens will weigh and slow you down, wear you out, and even affect your balance.

REVERSED MEANING

Don't hesitate for too long. If your thinking gets too involved, you will get yourself into a tangle.

Issue: Hesitancy.

Advice: Are you stuck? Is there any unfinished business? Old dreams are haunting you—dive deep into them and ask them what they still have to say to you before they will leave you alone. Don't let past grudges and grievances spread their poison into the future.

SEVEN OF SWORDS

Väinämöinen and Ilmarinen shuffle lots and ask the lots where the sun and moon have disappeared to.

When things aren't going according to plan, it is worth withdrawing for a while and seeking advice before moving on.

Issue: It is time to take stock of the situation.

Advice: Things aren't going according to plan. You try and try again. Nothing seems to be going smoothly. Are you going to run away? If so, then leave things in such a way that you are able to return to them. This won't be the last of this particular problem.

REVERSED MEANING

You are stubbornly hanging on to things and it is taking all your strength to do so. You have been given bad advice and it has led you astray. Advice is good or bad according to its appropriateness to the whole situation.

Issue: Seemingly good advice can still be inappropriate.

Advice: Listen carefully, because you might be given some advice or a few handy hints which could help you. Listen and think and, if need be, wait. Sometimes time is the only solution.

EIGHT OF SWORDS

When Väinämöinen, Lemminkäinen and Ilmarinen had robbed the Sampo, Louhi, the Mistress of Pohjola, asked Iku-Turso, the sea monster, to pursue them.

Fear has now got the upper hand. This distorts the situation in such a way that nothing can be solved, or even seen clearly, until the fear has been dealt with.

Issue: Panic, a crisis.

Advice: Nothing can be solved when you are blind-folded with your hands tied behind your back. Fear distorts reality. Distress can make you ill.

REVERSED MEANING

Once fear no longer rules your life you will have space in it for others, for your work, and above all, for yourself. However, until the situation you are in is resolved, you will continue to blame others for the fear and discomfort that is inside you. These other people are innocent, but you see your fear mirrored in their faces, in their actions and in their very beings. You imagine that they are against you and perhaps some of them are—you yourself have turned them against you.

Issue: Circumstances are against you.

Advice: Can you feel how those bonds from the past are loosening their grip on you—you will very soon be free of them. Things will change drastically. You will have time for yourself, for plans and activities.

NINE OF SWORDS

Louhi, the Mistress of Pohjola, sends terrible diseases to Kalevala as revenge for the robbery of the Sampo. The wise Väinämöinen dispels all the sickness, having first found out how it came about. It is essential to know the root of an evil in order to disempower it. This is not the same as allocating blame. It is just that the evil will reappear if it is not severed at the roots.

Issue: The root of an evil.

Advice: You have been cruel and heartless and now you are feeling remorse, guilt and anxiety. You wonder whether you should have left the deed undone. You blame yourself, yet now is the time for pity and forgiveness. There is always a time of sorrow when someone or something has been left behind.

REVERSED MEANING

True recovery can only happen once the cause of the sickness is located. It is useless to allocate blame, but another person can sometimes help you identify the dark areas in yourself. It is by far more fruitful to look inside yourself—you are the only person you can ever expect to change.

Issue: Evading the real reasons for something.

Advice: Tomorrow brings with it new hope and promise. Be ready for the sunshine. Don't hide in the shadows once it shines in on your life. Right now hope and faith are what you most need. Remember the saying, "It is always darkest before the day dawneth."

TEN OF SWORDS

Kullervo killed himself because he could no longer find anyone to seek his revenge on—he therefore turned in on himself. One of the tragedies of the human situation is that we never can return to the past—it is lost and gone forever. We can only be open to the new challenges that the present brings us—and ready to begin all over again what we have left undone. The old must perish and pride must be defeated. Any guilt, self-pity, and blame is futile.

Issue: "The last straw."

Advice: The past is lost—all the hopes and dreams you had are gone forever. Still, you cling to it desperately. You will never recapture the magic of yesterday—it will only hurt you all the more if you even try to do so.

REVERSED MEANING

The winds of change are blowing and you are coming alive again. Now it is time to forgive yourself and others for past mistakes. That will mean that the past has finally lost its last hold on you. It is good to be at peace, to accept that there is no longer any use in mulling over and over what happened. The way forward is to work through and come out on the other side of those thought patterns.

Issue: To come to a conclusion about something.

Advice: You have been through a hard time. The very structure of your life has been shattered. Now times are changing and everything and anything will be possible for you. There is nothing to hold you back any more. The sky is the limit.

KAUKOMIELI'S BLADE

ACCORDING TO THE KALEVALA, poems were also found on the tip of Kaukomieli's blade. The blade is a sword that Lemminkäinen had with him in all his battles, but which he hid under the cottage floor once he got back home again. Lemminkäinen was one of the Kalevala's main heroes. He was a good soldier and a womanizer. He wreaked havoc wherever he went.

A person's passion and creative will are the driving forces behind them. Fire is symbolic of will and determination in their purest forms. There is an old Finnish saying: "A strong will will take you through the grayest of stones." Kaukomieli's blade represents the element of fire. It corresponds to the stakes in a conventional tarot deck.

KAUKOMIELI'S BLADE

Lightning strikes the Earth and a great creative force springs forth. As of yet it has no definite form—it is a frightening and chaotic primeval force, pushing upwards just as the buds do in spring.

Issue: Willpower will lead to greatness.

Advice: New things are coming into being. New beginnings and new possibilities are opening before you. These will change your future direction. Try something new at work or at home; or find new ways to spend your free time.

REVERSED MEANING

Restlessness, an overflow of energy, which might manifest itself in either over-excitement or in fatigue brought about by the need to keep oneself under tight control.

Issue: Restlessness and an overflow of energy.

Advice: Don't give up yet. Bide your time and try to bear with your feelings—something new is only just beginning to take shape. Perhaps this would be a good time to cancel any unnecessary appointments and look into yourself for a while—find out what you really want. Anxiety is often a birthing pain of the creative process.

TWO OF STAKES

Lemminkäinen misses the excitement of battle.

Our will looks for a goal, an opportunity to act and to create. A force finds its polar force and the attraction is magnetic, the excitement feverish. The two snake torches show the two wills courting each other. Between them the sea, the amniotic fluid of creation, moves. A human being has a desire, a will driving him or her toward a goal over a sea of uncertainty. Will s/he get there, or will the waves of the sea engulf her or him?

Issue: What are the targets or goals?

Advice: There are new things happening, plans in the making— set yourself a target. You CAN succeed. Now is the time for discussion, the time to seek advice and come to agreements. Your will has manifested itself in a clear decision—courage will give you the strength and the faith to see things through.

REVERSED MEANING

You are over-excited and a bit too sure about the new targets or goals you have set yourself. Perhaps you should think again before you act—it is important to be realistic.

Issue: A sense of false security and over-excitement over new targets and goals.

Advice: Check the details of your plan of action. Go over the plan again and concentrate on it! Don't let anyone else influence your decision, but do make sure you give yourself enough time to make a good decision. Try and get your personal life in order, too.

THREE OF STAKES

Väinämöinen, Joukahainen and Aino are in competition; there are three forces and three wills at work. An aspiration is a desire for something, an attempt is what someone does to get it, and a decision is what brings the attempt about. Väinämöinen and Joukahainen have competed to see who is the strongest and most knowledgeable. The prize is the innocent maiden, Aino. Aino knows nothing of what is to be her fate.

Issue: Aspirations, attempts and decisions.

Advice: Someone is offering to help you. Make sure you are clear in your own vision of what you want, then see if there is anyone else around you who is on the same wavelength. Don't accept help or advice from anyone who isn't.

REVERSED MEANING

All participants have their own agenda. They are all going to lose out, because not one of them will relent and try to work with the others.

Issue: Everyone has their own agenda.

Advice: Skills, strengths and efforts are wasted, because the direction you are going in isn't clear. You need to set yourself more definite goals and to apply your skills more appropriately. Don't give up, however. Do try again! And don't be too proud to ask for encouragement.

FOUR OF STAKES

Ilmarinen weds the Pohjola Maiden. The wedding takes place both in Pohjola and in Kalevala. Thus, the two parties are joined in such a way that everyone is included. In a marriage a couple commit themselves to sharing their lives and to working toward the same goals.

Issue: Commitment.

Advice: The goal is set and your vision of it is crystal clear. You have a plan of action. That being so, now is the time for putting it into practice. You have reason to be pleased with yourself. A romance may lead to marriage.

REVERSED MEANING

Your misfortunes have led you to question whether this really is what you want. If so, then you need to decide so again, as doing this will renew your strength and help you carry on.

Issue: Do you really want to carry on with this?

Advice: Things will be looking up shortly. You have, after all, already made considerable progress and things will soon start moving again. Do tell those you care about what is going on.

FIVE OF STAKES

Lemminkäinen is at loggerheads with women. They all have their own expectations of him. Each one of them wants Lemminkäinen for herself. Similarly, people have expectations of you. They want you to fulfill them. All the people in your life have their own agendas for you, and these might be quite different from what you want for yourself. This results in a battle of wills.

Issue: Conflict. Everyone wants something different.

Advice: You are fighting and arguing with the people in your life. They don't want what you want for yourself, and are trying to persuade you to see things differently and to change your plans. This is a battle about priorities.

REVERSED MEANING

Silence is a form of giving in. People have accepted that you are going for what you want. They give you their silent support, but are, all the while, waiting for their turn. They know that your faith in them and their support will eventually work in their favor.

Issue: Friends are using the predicament you are in for their own gain.

Advice: Beware of silence. Things are bubbling under the surface. People have seemingly given you their support, but some of them are just biding their time and will seize any opportunity to do things their way. Try to communicate more with the people in your life and to let people have their say.

SIX OF STAKES

Lemminkäinen has caught the elk, the steed and the swan that Louhi demanded of him in exchange for her daughter's hand. It requires determination and single-mindedness in order to achieve one's goals—without these they easily slip out of reach.

Issue: You have done what you set out to do.

Advice: You need to believe in yourself—it is OK to win and you may well do it! There is nothing to stop you from succeeding now. Things are progressing smoothly. Some good news awaits.

REVERSED MEANING

Often there is a tendency to relax just a minute too soon, just before you are actually there—this could result in never getting there. Something has changed the situation you are in, and you need to look out or else you might have to begin all over again.

Issue: You are nearly there.

Advice: Are you sure you want to succeed? What would happen if you did? There is a part of you that is frightened of success. There will be new demands on you once you succeed, new targets and goals to aim for. Yesterday will be lost—there will be no return to what you know now, it will be lost and gone forever.

SEVEN OF STAKES

Lemminkäinen has come to Pohjola, only to find an iron fence around it. He doesn't know how to move forward, and yet the last thing he feels he can do is to go back. Lemminkäinen is stuck between the devil and the deep blue sea.

Issue: There are obstacles in your way, but there is no return. You are stuck.

Advice: You have inner strength. Your faith and willpower will see you through. Problems don't stay with you for long, because you look for a solution to them as soon as possible. You work well under pressure.

REVERSED MEANING

When the demands on you escalate and are added to the many former obligations you are under, it is easy to withdraw from the fight and to blame others for your predicament.

Issue: The past holds you to blame and the future puts demands on you.

Advice: Find the strength inside you. You tend to wait for something or someone to push you into doing something. Fear holds you back and blinds you to your own strength. Look your fear in the eye and don't let it persuade you that you are weak. Be patient with yourself, yet move forward, if slowly and surely, in the direction you set out in—don't be misled into sudden changes of mind.

EIGHT OF STAKES

Lemminkäinen carries off Kyllikki and drives her home in his sledge to be his wife.

Once the talking is over, the goals are clear and the targets decided on, it is time for action and time to do what is necessary, regardless of momentary whims and desires.

Issue: Nothing can stop you now.

Advice: Things are moving very quickly. Things are going according to plan. You are teeming with new ideas that all enhance your original one. This is a time of activity, movement, and important events.

REVERSED MEANING

Your fear is standing in the way of necessary activity. It is making you think, even though it is time to act. Your insecurity is gnawing at you, paralyzing you. Hence, the situation is becoming more and more complicated—things are tying themselves into knots. You will miss your chance.

Issue: A chance is lost.

Advice: Fear and insecurity go hand in hand. Insecurity gives rise to turmoil. Turmoil erodes all foundations, giving rise to more insecurity. Try and keep a strong hold on your feelings, as there will be arguments and jealousies. Keep your cool—acting in haste and out of distress may spoil everything for you.

NINE OF STAKES

After felling the Elk of Hiisi, Lemminkäinen crawls inside it. He wants, somehow, to have some of the elk's power—to overcome his fears and to be one with the creatures of the forest. A person has to become one with what s/he wants, to surrender him or herself to it. A person becomes what s/he has wished for.

Issue: Having something means becoming something.

Advice: Concentrate on holding your own. Be very careful that you don't lose out in your dealings with others. So far you have done well. Listen to people. Protect yourself. It is good to keep your strong will hidden under an unassuming demeanor. However, do give others an indication of how determined you can be.

REVERSED MEANING

You are trying, by using brute force, to conquer something that won't be cowed no matter what. It will only gain in strength the more you fight it.

Issue: Fighting this will only make it stronger.

Advice: Your intuition and sensitivity are lost under your brutality. Don't bite off your nose to spite your face. Abandon yourself to the situation without losing sight of your own goals. Be prepared to take orders. Fight for your principles, fight for truth and justice.

TEN OF STAKES

Trees were once felled and whole forests burned to make fields. Trees were sacrificed to make way for harvests. You must let go of the old before the new can be born.

Issue: Things are crystallizing—a decision is being made.

Advice: You have faced many challenges and been working under considerable pressure for some time now. Things are beginning to take shape at last. What are you going to do next? Beware of burning out. Everything is under control, but you are vulnerable and there is still some way to go. It could be that you will need to make a few more decisions before you can finalize things.

REVERSED MEANING

The past still has a hold on you. You still aren't ready to let it go. You are stuck because of something that you used to want very much.

Issue: Clinging on to the old.

Advice: You are using your skills, knowledge and creativity in a way that is detrimental to yourself. You are trying to juggle with many things and the balls are flying everywhere. You need to put things in order of priority for yourself and to make your priorities clear to others. Do something about this—now.

THE MOORS OF KALEVA

Poems were also found on the Kaleva moors, where Väinämöinen, Lemminkäinen, and Ilmarinen lived. In the Kalevala Tarot, the dish cards represent the moors—the moors being the homestead, the place where we feel we most belong and which we always long to return to, no matter what. We feel good in the familiar landscape of our childhood and we are happiest when walking along our childhood paths. The Kaleva moors correspond to the tarot cups and the element of water.

THE MOORS OF KALEVA

In the past, stories and tales were told of an evening. They were a way of passing time, of relaxing and being entertained. They were also a means of bringing meaning and continuity into daily activities, and of both expressing and influencing emotions. Once a task or an event is given meaning, our lives become more worthwhile and, therefore, happier. Our minds project forth feelings and these are shown in our faces, in our expressions (or lack of them). Our faces are the homes of our feelings. They are the Kaleva moors of our bodies, from whence we can endeavor to decipher some of a person's inner life.

Issue: There are many ways to influence the emotions.

Advice: This is the beginning of many good things to come. There is love, health, and happiness in store for you. Rejoice! The new beginning is a blessed one. The emotional side of your life is coming to the forefront and you will be enriched immensely by this.

REVERSED MEANING

Happiness never seems to come your way. It is hard to find any joy or inspiration in your surroundings—you have, as Hamlet had, "lost all your mirth." You are depressed. Life is boring, dull, sad, and predictable.

Issue: There are pent-up emotions.

Advice: You are behaving in a selfish and self-centered way. Cast your selfishness aside and see how others react. You are sullen, fed up, and bored. Look further into yourself to find more meaning in your life.

TWO OF DISHES

Aino and Väinämöinen met among the birch trees and spoke with one another. Väinämöinen fell for Aino. A relationship is beginning. You are infatuated with each other. You give to each other of the abundant joy and happiness you each have because of the other. At this stage it isn't wise to get too serious about the relationship.

Issue: A budding romance.

Advice: There is a deep understanding between the two of you. There is a mutual giving and taking of love and friendship. Together you become something more than just two separate individuals. There is a harmony between you. This is a very good start to a romance, relationship, or friendship.

REVERSED MEANING

Things from the outside are penetrating your bubble-for-two. It is important to talk about them and to reach a compromise about them.

Issue: Reality is bursting your bubble.

Advice: You are arguing about irrelevant issues and creating mountains out of molehills. There will be a way forward, but one of you will have to make the first move. Until that happens, there will be more and more misunderstandings. Do stick together and try to understand the other one's perception of the problems, as this might lead to new solutions. Otherwise, you might lose a friendship, partner, or lover.

THREE OF DISHES

Kyllikki was the daughter of wealthy parents. She enjoyed herself with the other girls. She was beautiful; so beautiful that the sun, the moon, and the stars, all in turn, wooed her for their sons. Kyllikki was also a good dancer. She was the mistress of all that brought about joy and delight. When this card is picked, it shows that it is now time for pleasure, for laughter and rejoicing. Now is the time to be frolicking. Laughter and happiness are the soil in which new ideas and possibilities are nourished and blossom forth, just as in springtime the flowers push up out of the earth, and the future looks brighter for it.

Issue: Celebration and rejoicing.

Advice: A time of success, happiness, rejoicing and pleasure. Something amazing is about to happen. The future looks bright. Celebration is in the air. Sometimes pleasure is a good investment. Perhaps there will be a party.

REVERSED MEANING

Others may feel jealous when they see a joyful face and a happy smile—they feel excluded. Perhaps they are stuck in a bad place in their own lives. Soon you, too, become downcast—as if the negative feelings are contagious.

Issue: Curbing your joy.

Advice: What is of joy today will bring sorrow tomorrow. After the sun, the rain; and after the rain, the sun. Don't bank too much on the source of your joy—direct your attention to other people and channel your energies into several things.

FOUR OF DISHES

Ilmatar dwelt for a long time on the outermost edges of the Cosmos. Then, one day, she descended into the sea and was rocked in the cradle of the waves for a while until she became pregnant. She gave birth to Väinämöinen. Rest, peace, and relaxation do not mean that you are being lazy—it is just that you need to bide your time; a lot is happening under the surface. Don't be impatient. Just enjoy your time of relaxation and the fact that you are alive, here and now. Let your thoughts wander wherever they need to; you've got time to think. Use your time of waiting to the full.

Issue: Peace of mind.

Advice: A time of monotony, repetition and boredom. You lack motivation. Things have been too easy for you and you are spoiled. You should push yourself more. No one seems to want to understand you right now.

REVERSED MEANING

Doing nothing can be creative, as ideas and thoughts might be ripening inside you. You do need to be clear about when you are actually being lazy, though. Then you will better be able to enjoy just *being* when it is right for you to do so.

Issue: Laziness, apathy.

Advice: Slowly you are emerging out of your shell and beginning to put things in order. There might be a surprise in store for you that will break the monotony and the waiting. You just might make a new acquaintance, too.

FIVE OF DISHES

A bride-to-be is told that she must leave her childhood home and the things of her youth behind her. Her elders speak with her, reminding her of what she must leave when she sets up home together with her husband, and often reducing her to tears. She must put the past behind her—its joys as well as its sorrows. There is indeed sadness in letting things go. You can't take the past with you—it has to be grieved over in order to make room for the future. Old friends make way for new friends. A topic or a subject that used to engage your attention may lose its fascination for you.

Issue: Rejection.

Advice: There is a raging storm inside you and you wish to be free of it. However, grieving is a process—be patient with yourself. Remember that when you turn toward one person you turn your back on another. Think hard about who you wish to turn to and who you can turn away from.

REVERSED MEANING

Things will start improving once you no longer cling to the past. A whole new world will open up before you. New interests and new people will help you find the impetus and the courage you need to heal your broken heart.

Issue: Clinging to the past.

Advice: Things are looking up—it wasn't the end of the world after all. A new world has opened out before you, and courage has entered your broken heart once more.

SIX OF DISHES

Väinämöinen got shot at by Joukahainen. He fell into the water. Eventually, an eagle carried him to the Pohjola shores. Louhi, the Pohjola mistress, took him in.

"Do to others as you would be done by" is the message of this card. All of us can do something for others. We should care for those who aren't as well off as we are. If you feel hard done by, seek out others who have even less and try your best to help them.

Issue: Alleviating need, creating comfort.

Advice: Memories of the past are surfacing. You might be reunited with an old friend. The renewal of a friendship cheers you and fills you with renewed hope. There is happiness in fond memories.

REVERSED MEANING

The appreciation of your good services or all your efforts goes to someone else. You don't get the thanks or the recognition you deserve. You probably feel cheated and frustrated. Be assertive about what is your due—make yourself heard!

Issue: Someone else gets the credit that should be yours.

Advice: There are complications and hold-ups over something you've been longing for. Perhaps some attention you should have been given is either given to someone else, or it is a long time coming. The delay really puts you to the test—what are your real motives and how true are your feelings about this issue? Do bide your time.

SEVEN OF DISHES

Väinämöinen, after all he had been through, went in search of his kantele, which had been lost in the water. He didn't find it and returned home disconsolate.

Something that really used to enthrall you has lost its magic. It now seems mundane and unexciting. The joys of yesterday are often disappointments today.

Issue: Disappointments.

Advice: Reaching a decision is never easy. Making choices is an agonizing undertaking. When you begin to feel that you can't see the wood for the trees, it is time to take a break and leave things to rest for a while. Something that used to satisfy and even inspire you no longer does. Old sources of feeling no longer resonate for you. You need to explore something new.

REVERSED MEANING

Now is the time for single-mindedness. Don't give in to temptation. Your actions will get you to your goal and success will be waiting for you there. Keep a vision in your mind of what it is you have been working so hard for. Your work will be rewarded, but only once it is completed.

Issue: Working for something is more rewarding than having it handed to you on a silver platter.

Advice: Keep your goal in mind. Be careful not to be led astray by too many questions and suggestions at this point. You will succeed if you don't let your determination flag or let passing temptations get the better of you. The right career will bring you what you are hoping for.

EIGHT OF DISHES

Väinämöinen goes fishing for Aino. He catches a big fish who tells him she is Aino.

You are living in the past. Your memories are taking over today and standing in the way of the new. You long to relive, if only for a moment, past joys. You feel it was all over too soon, before it had been fully lived through, and it lives on in the longing in your heart.

Issue: Reliving the past.

Advice: Once you have reached a certain goal, rested there and enjoyed it for a while, then the time has come to move on. You need to challenge yourself in a completely different way, in order to find what you are looking for.

REVERSED MEANING

Where have your feelings gone? You aren't giving them any say at all right now. You are being sensible and reasonable to the detriment of your feelings.

Issue: Numbed feelings.

Advice: You are concentrating too much on the material comforts in your life. There is more to life than your surroundings than where you are at the moment. What about you—your inner being and your need to grow? You need to be striving for something you believe in—look into yourself with a view to uncovering what that could be.

NINE OF DISHES

Väinämöinen made a kantele from the jaws of a huge pike. He makes such wonderful music with it that all living things come to hear him.

Dreams can come true. True happiness comes from listening to your own inner voice. Speaking it will make others listen, too. You will feel more satisfied than ever before and find fulfillment you have not yet known.

Issue: Finding and listening to your own inner voice.

Advice: Dreams do come true. You now have everything you want. Your needs are more than fulfilled, and you have no worries. Enjoy the abundance!

REVERSED MEANING

This time it looks as if you won't get what you what you were hoping for. There is still a lot to be pleased about. However, it is hard for you to appreciate that at the moment, focused as you are on the one thing you didn't get. Once you are over your disappointment, you will find contentment after all.

Issue: In time, you will be content.

Advice: You realize your dream. However, don't underestimate what you have got. Are you looking for consolation in all the wrong places? What you were longing for might never be yours, but don't disregard what you *have* achieved and what *is* yours. Take comfort in these and don't settle for second best in something, the best of which you couldn't have.

TEN OF DISHES

Out in the forest, watching over the sheep, Marjatta swallows a cranberry and becomes pregnant.

There can be great happiness in the smallest of things. There will be plenty of sources of such happiness in your life, too. A small thing might be the very stimulus that fills you with such emotions as you have been missing out on and waiting for all your life.

Issue: The seeds of happiness are small.

Advice: You are happy. You have got what you hoped for. You are at peace with yourself and your surroundings. Happiness is your due now, so allow yourself to enjoy it. Let it glow in you, flow through you; listen to it.

REVERSED MEANING

Trivialities irritate you. You are making mountains out of molehills and they are blocking out happiness. It is even hard to do and enjoy the things you generally like. You feel you are bursting with negative feelings.

Issue: You have made a mountain out of a molehill.

Advice: Your surroundings seem bleak and austere. You are in the swamp of depression and you are stuck. You can't even begin to imagine that you could ever feel happy or joyful or loving again. The winds of change will soon be blowing—let them take you to where you will, once more, feel love and joy flowing through you.

THE FIELDS OF POHJOLA

Poems were also to be found on the fields of Pohjola. In Pohjola, which represents the material, the concrete world, what counts is what we own—either a little or a lot. The value of our possessions is measured in money and our status or position in society determines how we behave. Possessions are a way of protecting ourselves. However, possessions need protection, too—the size of a field, the quality and quantity of a harvest, are all things which have been fought over.

Pohjola is described as being a cold, dreary, dark and evil place. The Fields of Pohjola best correspond to the coins in a conventional deck of tarot cards, and in the Kalevala Tarot are represented by loaves. The element they best represent is earth.

THE FIELDS OF POHJOLA

A Kalevala bride-to-be is well-prepared for her life in a new home. Before the wedding, she is given much advice on such matters as how to behave as a daughter-in-law, and later on, perhaps a mistress of her own household. She is told about her work in detail.

This is the beginning of prosperity. There will be a new acquisition soon. A good foundation brings about good results.

Issue: A new start.

Advice: You will prosper and thrive. At long last everything will be sorted out. Do remember that it is safest to build on a good foundation. You will be getting something new, something you've been waiting for. Perhaps you will be rewarded unexpectedly—you might be the recipient of an important book or document.

REVERSED MEANING

It is important to concentrate on the new possibilities before you, rather than to celebrate them—that time will come later. Things might not go according to plan and you may have to have a rethink. However, if things are already running seemingly smoothly, leave well enough alone—chopping and changing would only complicate matters at this stage.

Issue: Difficulty in getting started.

Advice: You have a false sense of security. Your plans might yet fail. Turn your attention to the things you've been neglecting, such as the needs of others. Your money and possessions have made a prisoner of you. Think again—perhaps you have chosen badly.

TWO OF LOAVES

The dogs bark when Väinämöinen comes into the yard of the Pohjola household. The Pohjola Master asks his daughter to go and have a look to see who it is, but she doesn't have the time as she is busy with her chores and her baking.

We are in a time of flux. This is when people cling to routines, to the chores and work of the everyday. Still, times change, slowly and surely. It takes time to prepare and make way for the new.

Issue: The past is behind us, yet the new is not yet before us.

Advice: You are trying to sit in two chairs at once. You obviously can't be in two places at the same time! Things will be a lot easier once you have made a decision.

REVERSED MEANING

You are very afraid of change. Don't give in to your fear. It will recede as the new begins to take shape. What you need is to decide what your focus is going to be on in the things to come.

Issue: Slowly but surely things will come to a head.

Advice: The old ways of doing things have lost their meaning. This feels threatening and confusing at first. Don't be too hard on yourself if things don't go according to plan the first time round. Encourage yourself to give things another try.

THREE OF LOAVES

Ilmarinen forges the magical Sampo which brings forth happiness, success and riches for whoever is in possession of it. Once you are in possession of skills, knowledge and resources, it is time to get to work. This work will bring with it new possibilities, possibilities which it is in your power to make work for or against you.

Issue: This is work for a professional.

Advice: You have got what it takes and there is plenty to do. There is no doubt that you could be a great success if only you concentrate on the task at hand. Your efforts won't go unnoticed. You will be valued at your place of work or by experts in your field.

REVERSED MEANING

Your work isn't progressing as it should. You need to make more of an effort—after all, part of what working is about is focusing on a given task and giving it your all. Work and pulling your weight in the things you have committed yourself to must be a priority right now.

Issue: The work has to be done, and to a satisfactory standard.

Advice: Your work isn't going well. You need to acquire more skills and more experience. You need more practice at whatever it is you do—practice makes perfect. Don't expect results yet. There are going to be some delays. Don't give up—show the world that you have staying power. Remember—you can't speed up the flow of a river!

FOUR OF LOAVES

The magical Sampo is stored in Pohjola behind nine locks within the Mount of Copper.

You now own something which you feel is the source of your well-being and success. This may well be the case—it depends entirely on you and whether you use it wisely.

Issue: To maintain and protect what is yours.

Advice: The material world means a lot to you. It is important to go by what you feel and what you believe in. Just be clear about what belongs where and to whom. Then protect and care for what is yours: your home, your money and your possessions. Don't squander what you already have.

REVERSED MEANING
Someone is trying to rob you of what is rightfully yours. Or perhaps your capital is trickling away because it is being neglected. It is very important to be clear about who owns what and who stands to gain from it.

Issue: Who owns what, and who will gain from that?

Advice: Someone is trying to rob you of something. Your capital or something precious to you is being wasted, either by being put to bad use or by not being used at all. It is time to put down boundaries—to be clear about what is and isn't yours, about what you are the rightful owner of, and also about the things not a single one of us has the right to own.

FIVE OF LOAVES

Lemminkäinen's home burns down and his mother is forced to flee. Lemminkäinen seeks revenge. Kullervo burns the homestead of Untamo in revenge, because he believes Untamo has killed all other members of the Kalervo clan to which Kullervo belongs.

The grass is always greener on the other side of the fence—those on the outside want in, and those on the inside want out. Sometimes people try to get to the other side of the fence by using brute force. This will invariably lead to bitterness, which, in turn, will lead to someone seeking counter-revenge one day. Creation and destruction are eternal cycles, as are life and death.

Issue: Redundancy.

Advice: Clarify your position to yourself. What is on the inside and what is on the outside? You might feel that you are an outsider, different maybe, unconventional in some way, and excluded. Circumstances sometimes change. All you can do is to carry on with your chosen path.

REVERSED MEANING

You are being excluded and, maybe, even banished from your home and a community that has meant much to you. You have grown and had to leave behind you a world that has become too small for you, and yet was very secure. You are like a bird leaving its cozy nest—the sky is, indeed, the limit!

Issue: There just isn't room for everyone, so some people will be excluded.

Advice: Accept the circumstances as much as you can. Try to learn from them. Try to adapt. There will be changes—don't reject these.

SIX OF LOAVES

The wife of Ilmarinen makes Kullervo her herdsman, and gives him a loaf of bread to take with him.

Rather than destroy the old, why not pass it on to another to whom it may be of use? Where there is more than enough, what is extraneous should be given away—this creates a balance. The giver gains as much from this balance as the receiver does.

Issue: There is more than enough and something can be given away.

Advice: Things are going well, and you have all and more than you need. At this point in time your role in life is that of a giver. Share out what you've got fairly, so as to be of benefit to as many people as possible. Have no fear—by giving now you will not lose out. All that you give to others, and more, will one day be returned to you.

REVERSED MEANING

There is always someone who feels that life owes them something, whether s/he will give of him or herself to life or not. Perhaps you are in a position to share what you have with such an individual; however, they probably won't be any happier for it—what you have isn't necessarily what they want.

Issue: There will always be takers.

Advice: You expect someone to give you what you need. Are you sure you deserve it? The gift you received doesn't live up to your expectations. You are envious of those who are better off than you.

SEVEN OF LOAVES

Kullervo lived in Untamo's house. Kullervo made a mess of things, so Untamo sells Kullervo to Ilmarinen as a slave.

It is harvesting time. Take stock of what you have achieved. It could all be either for the good or the bad.

Issue: What has been accomplished?

Advice: You have done well. Take stock of what you have achieved so far and enjoy it for a while. After that, it will be time to think about how you are going to make your achievements work for you. What will you do next? These achievements have brought you a step closer to your ultimate goal.

REVERSED MEANING

You are disappointed, because the results weren't as good as you had hoped they would be. You do not see the outcome of all your great efforts.

Issue: What is the outcome of all your good work?

Advice: You may well be disappointed, as the results of your efforts are not what you expected. You expected much more of something completely different. You are puzzled—this wasn't supposed to happen, and you don't know what to do. You should make the most of what you've got.

EIGHT OF LOAVES

As Ilmarinen had lost his wife, he decided to forge himself a new one of gold and silver. Having done so, he sleeps beside her and finds her cold and unpleasant.

Results, accomplishments, and goals are the raw materials, the stepping stones to get us to where we want to be. We have to work: work to get there, work at being there, work at appreciating what we have worked for and at finding new avenues for growth and self-improvement.

Issue: The harvest must be prepared for use.

Advice: You need to think about how you can best put what you have achieved to use. Is there anything that should be discarded? Things need constant revising. Not everything will be beneficial to your future plans.

REVERSED MEANING
If you don't feel satisfied with your achievements yet, then perhaps you need to look at ways of continuing to work on the same thing.

Issue: You aren't satisfied with what you've achieved so far.

Advice: The thought of carrying on fills you with anxiety and impatience. You feel weak, because you expect too much too soon. Concentrate on what you need to do today.

NINE OF LOAVES

The inhabitants of Pohjola lived carefree lives once the Sampo had been forged. There was great prosperity. No Pohjola dweller lacked for anything. In fact, everyone had more than they needed and could have shared it all with others.

Happy is the person who has enough. Enjoy it, and enjoy life. If you have more than enough, pass it on to others. Anything you have beyond what you need will only tie you down. It will stand in the way of the things you want for your future.

Issue: Give away what is left over.

Advice: You have feelings of inadequacy, even though you have all you need. You are looking for a challenge. People see your prosperity, but you feel your need and you know that something is missing from your life. You are secure in material terms, yet insecure mentally and emotionally. However, you are a very dutiful person and well able to look after yourself.

REVERSED MEANING
If you are unhappy it isn't because something is missing from your life, but because you have too much. This is standing in the way of new beginnings for you.

Issue: There is no room for the new in a place where there is already too much.

Advice: Have a fresh look at what it is you want, at what your hopes and aspirations are. Take time to look about you and to give others something you can be very generous with—your attention. Ask for help and advice, if need be, from those who are a bit further along your chosen path.

TEN OF LOAVES

The Sampo broke. Louhi takes a fragment of its cover back to Pohjola. Väinämöinen collects the other fragments and takes them with him to Kalevala, where he plants them, hoping they will bring good fortune to the Kaleva people.

Completion is when something has taken on such a shape that it can perpetuate growth and be a part of the great creative cycle.

Issue: Increased well-being.

Advice: You are there now, practically speaking. Soon you will be able to breathe a sigh of relief. You will feel safe. Your financial situation will be secure and this means you can concentrate on the other sides of your life. Now you can freely acknowledge that you've finally made it!

REVERSED MEANING

There is one setback after another. Nothing is going smoothly. Perhaps you are paying too much attention to the new, before the old is properly out of your hair. You need to get things to a place where they run smoothly without you, before you start doing something else.

Issue: See the work you are doing through to a place where it can carry on without you once you have moved on.

Advice: There is one setback after another. You are afraid you might fail. Not one thing is working as it should. You wish it was all over and done with, yet your motivation is flagging and laziness is setting in. Give yourself a mental shake, take stock of what the situation demands of you, and get on with it.

KALEVALA SPREADS

UKKO'S TOOLS

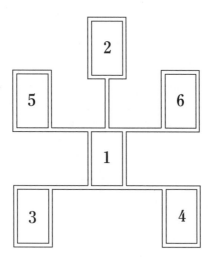

1. You are…
2. The question is…
3. The cause of this was…
4. What happened was…
5. The past has been…
6. The future will be…
7. Return to 1. Ask yourself what YOU will do about this.

1. THE QUESTIONER *Väinämöinen's belt*

The central character of the Kalevala is Väinämöinen. He was there at the beginning of time; he is the primeval sorcerer. He is involved in everything that happens in the Kalevala, if at times indirectly. The Kalevala poems and songs were born out of Väinämöinen's belt. The midriff is, as the name implies, a central part of a person's body—s/he can put a belt around it and then s/he will be, as it were, in the center of the belt. This is where a tarot consultation begins, with you in the center, as "Väinämöinen." This reading is about your particular song—the tarot cards tell us your story.

Your life can be looked at, either by going through the whole journey so far, or by looking at the situation you are in at present. Your journey through life, of course, has brought you here. This moment is where time and eternity meet. Perhaps you are with a diviner, perhaps you are alone and turning to the tarot for advice. Try to empty your mind and then lift the first card—it is about you.

2. THE QUESTION *Ilmarinen's forge*

Ilmarinen is another Kalevala hero. He is the primeval craftsman. He forged the very heavens. In the Kalevala, he is the one who gets things done. Whatever Väinämöinen couldn't do himself he got Ilmarinen to do for him. Ilmarinen forged the magical Sampo which brought riches, happiness, and well-being to whomever possessed it. The heavens of a human being are surely in her or his head, in which there are thoughts that s/he uses to understand concepts and create ideas.

A tarot consultation deals with the issues, ideas and questions a person may have. Often there is one particular issue in which s/he feels in need of advice. Like Ilmarinen, the person has possibly created something that turns out to be problematic, just as the Sampo was.

This reading will hopefully help you see things in a different light and to come up with new ideas and solutions. Just like

Ilmarinen, you will be able to craft into being a new perception of whatever it is you are having difficulties with. The reading can also be seen as a tool with which to create a better life for yourself. Empty your mind and lift the second card. This card will show you the question in the light of the Kalevala Tarot.

3. THE CAUSE *The Fields of Pohjola*
The place that caused the Kaleva people a whole lot of heart-ache was Pohjola. There was the Pohjola maiden whom the men dreamed about and desired. There was Louhi, the Mistress of Pohjola, who wanted the Sampo, put a curse on the Kaleva people when she had been robbed of it, and nursed Väinämöinen.

The Pohjola fields represent that mysterious place in a person which is the source of many of our problems. More often than not, an individual him or herself is the main cause of their woes. For all sorts of reasons s/he allows or causes things to happen which get him or her into tricky situations. The outside world becomes a projection of the inner reality.

This card endeavors to get to the bottom, or root, of what really is going on. Sometimes what seems to be the problem turns out to be a mere symptom of another, much deeper problem. This card delves deeper, in order to get to the core issues. This card can unmask you, see you for what you are and why you got into this particular situation. Finding guilty parties and allocating blame is not the intention—for that it would be more appropriate to hire a lawyer or a judge. What we are looking for is what the individual's part is in what has happened. That is something that s/he can do something about. Empty your mind and lift the third Kalevala Tarot card now.

4. WHAT HAPPENED *The Kaleva Moors*
The Kaleva people lived on the Kaleva moors. The moors were described as being the most wonderful place on earth. They were the home you happily returned to, time and again, from

your travels and adventures. They were where you rested, worked and played, where you kept house and company with the people you knew better than any others.

This card focuses on what it was that brought things to the surface, to a head. For example, neglecting to carry out your duties means that sooner or later your finances, your relationships or your peace of mind will be the worse for it. Empty your mind and lift the fourth card, where what happened will be seen in the light of the Kalevala Tarot.

5. THE PAST *Joukahainen's Bow*

Joukahainen was a young man who wanted to be the world's best at *everything*. He challenged Väinämöinen to a duel. Having lost the duel, Joukahainen seeks revenge and ends up shooting Väinämöinen off his horse.

A person's past is constantly seeking compensation, challenging the present to duels and standing in the way of the future. This card deals with the past, aiming to determine the influence of the past on the present situation. There may be unfinished business that needs to be worked through before the road to the future is clear. Empty your mind and lift the fifth Kalevala Tarot card, which will reveal to you the hold the past has on your future.

6. THE FUTURE *Kaukomieli's Blade*

Lemminkäinen, also known by the name Kaukomieli, is the third Kaleva Hero. Lemminkäinen's mother used to worry about him and warn him about being foolhardy. He is a warrior and a womanizer. He has a restless, adventurous nature and thrives on challenges. He is always on the move, always on to the next thing, always making plans for the day after tomorrow. This card looks at the future from the point of view of the questioner. This card deals with future plans, ambitions and goals—ones which the individual can work on. It can help you make them. This card also examines and reveals what is impossible, what cannot be. Empty your mind and lift the sixth card, your future.

7. THE RETURN Now that the areas where changes can be made have been located, we need to return to the beginning of the Kalevala Tarot consultation. Returning to the beginning, coming full circle and ending at the beginning, will complete the consultation. Can you identify a keyword or catchphrase that will help you keep in mind what you have learned from your consultation with the Kalevala Tarot? This word or phrase would be like a tool that you can use to shape your future.

CHOICES

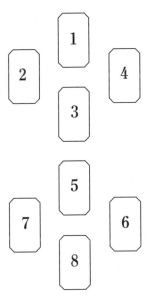

This spread will, as its name indicates, help you make choices. We are often confronted with offers, suggestions, and other matters that we need time to think over before we know whether or not we want to accept them. Once we have accepted something we often have a certain responsibility toward it, hence the importance of knowing our own minds.

1. Confrontation.
Before you accept the option, you say that you need time to think it over and will get back to it later. This card reveals the significance this particular option holds or will hold for you.

2. Rejection.
You reject the option without further thought. This is something you don't even want to consider. This card shows what lies behind your immediate reaction to this offer.
   Empty your mind and lift the second card.

3. You are considering it.
You feel that this option is worth considering. This card reveals exactly what it is you wish or need to consider.
   Empty your mind and lift the third card.

4. You reject the offer after considering it.
You have decided, after considerable thought, to reject the option—it just isn't right for you. The fourth card reveals what it really is that you will be giving up.
   Empty your mind and lift the fourth card.

5. Think about it one last time.
You need to think about it one more time, even though you were so sure at first that this wasn't what you wanted. Perhaps your immediate rejection was hasty and revealed to you certain aspects of your attitude that you want to explore a bit more. This fifth card helps you to do so.
   Empty your mind now and lift the fifth Kalevala Tarot card.

6. The positive aspects of the option.
You want to explore the benefits this choice could bring with it. With the sixth card as your guide you can consider the ways in which accepting this offer could enrich your life.
   Empty your mind and lift the sixth card.

When consulting the sixth and seventh cards, you could use a pen and paper and list all the negative aspects of the option on one side of it and the positive aspects on the other.

7. The negative aspects of the option.

If you wish to examine the negative aspects of the offer, you can do so with the help of the seventh card. This card will help you to explore all the drawbacks which an acceptance of the option would bring with it.

Empty your mind and lift the seventh card.

Have you made a note of all the negatives and positives on paper? Do the positives outweigh the negatives, or vice versa?

8. In front of you are now seven tarot cards and, possibly, a list of the negative and positive aspects involved in accepting this option. You can view the option from three different angles— the cards show it holistically, whereas the negatives and positives are singled out on paper. If you are ready to make a decision, then it is time to lift the eighth and final card. This card shows what the decision means, or symbolizes, to you.

Empty your mind and lift the final card.

After this it is advisable to put your decision in writing. Try and make it as short and concise as you can.

RELATIONSHIPS

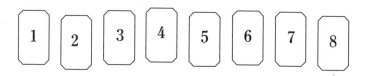

Relationships help a person to develop and teach him or her more about themselves than anything else ever could. In relating with others a personality is forged, just as iron was at Ilmarinen's forge. The character is worked on and refined in much the same way as Ilmarinen would work on and refine something he had crafted.

We can find ourselves, our friends and acquaintances described in the following cards—the very people (including, of course, ourselves) who are the cause of most of our trials and tribulations.

The First Card
Choose the card out of all the court cards (the ones in Ilmarinen's forge) that you feel most describes you in your relations with others. Place it on the table with the picture

side face up. (If you feel uncertain, you can let the tarot deck choose this card for you. This can be done by shuffling all the court cards thoroughly and by then picking a card with your left hand.)

The Second Card
Now either choose or pick a second card in the same way as you did the first. This card describes your companion. Place it next to the first card. Now you can, with the help of the cards, start a dialogue where the difficult issues gnawing at your relationship or friendship are explored. Look at the cards and let your thoughts wander freely over different aspects of the relationship. You could write down all that comes to mind.

Now shuffle the court or forge cards.

The Third Card
Pick a third card. This card represents the problem your friendship or relationship is facing.

The Fourth Card
Pick a fourth card. This card helps you to find a different way of approaching the problem. Perhaps, for example, the whole thing should just be written off and no longer allowed to come between you? Let your thought associations run freely. You might find it useful to write them down.

The Fifth Card
Pick the fifth card. This card gives an indication of the significance of what comes between you. Perhaps it is a detail, of little significance, or perhaps it is or will be fundamental to your whole relationship.

The Sixth Card
Pick the sixth card. This relates to your feelings right now. You might be feeling bad, or guilty, or indifferent about the whole affair.

The Seventh Card

Pick the seventh card. This card may help you to think of ways forward and out of the stalemate. Can you think of suggestions to put to your companion, or of anything you could do to alleviate the situation?

Finally, you could think over the following suggestions:

▷ Are you able to talk this or these matters over with your companion? If so, do you think your relationship will benefit from resolving this or these issues? If not, then what else could you do? Would it be advisable to ask a third party for help?

▷ Can you think of anything else that would make for better relations between the two of you?

▷ The negative has very much been in the forefront—can you think of anything you find positive about all of this?

Take a moment to concisely write down any conclusions or insights this consultation has left you with.

NOTES

NOTES